Yellow Flesh / Alabaster Rose

Plays by Erik Patterson

Tonseisha

Yellow Flesh / Alabaster Rose

Red Light, Green Light

He Asked For It

Sick

I Wanna Hold Your Hand

One of the Nice Ones

Handjob

Books by Erik Patterson

Pop Prompts: 200 Writing Prompts Inspired by Popular Music

Pop Prompts For Swifties: 99 Writing Prompts

Praise for *Yellow Flesh / Alabaster Rose*

"Erik Patterson's strange new play is one that takes you by surprise and ravishes you... He's clearly a playwright with more on his mind than the naturalistic details and fraught comedy of dysfunctional relationships, both of which he nails when he gets around to it. It's the getting-around-to-it part that shows Patterson's formal and philosophical ambitions..."

—Rob Kendt, *Backstage West*

"Daring in its frank approach to the subject matter and mesmerizing in its skillful blend of ironic humor and stark tragedy."

—Les Spindle, *Frontiers Magazine*

"*Yellow Flesh/Alabaster Rose* is so bold and imaginative and clever in the way it, and the characters, transcend the horror [of sexual abuse] that it comes off, triumphantly, as real. The playwright Erik Patterson has a wonderful ear for dialogue, and his characters never sound phony, even in their kinkiest moments... [The play is] an eloquent testament to the redemptive power of truth, and the tyranny of secrets and lies."

—Greg Owen, *In Los Angeles Magazine*

"A sublime meditation on the psychic injuries of incest, and how to heal them... An effortless intermingling of introspective drama and very funny comedy."

—Martin Hernandez, *LA Weekly*

"Packs a considerable emotional wallop, not to mention a hefty quotient of mordant wit."

—F. Kathleen Foley, *Los Angeles Times*

"Patterson manages to grip us with the obvious pathos while, at the same time, daring us to laugh. And we do, a lot. The drama of the piece is filled with embarrassed laughter, scandalized snickers, comic relief, chuckles of disbelief, and just plain humor—all of it dark."

—Dave DePino, *ShowMag.com*

Yellow Flesh / Alabaster Rose

by Erik Patterson

Camden High Street Books
2023

My Favorite Things
from THE SOUND OF MUSIC
Lyrics by Oscar Hammerstein II
Music by Richard Rodgers
Copyright © 1959 Williamson Music Company c/o Concord Music Publishing
Copyright Renewed
All Rights Reserved Used by Permission
Reprinted by Permission of Hal Leonard LLC

Print ISBN: 979-8-9878016-8-0
eBook ISBN: 979-8-9882250-0-3

Library of Congress Control Number: 2023907678
First Paperback Edition, May 2023

Copy editing by Sherry Angel
Cover image by Vidar Nordii-Mathisen
Back cover image by Majid Rangraz

Printed in the United States of America
Los Angeles, CA
www.erikpatterson.org

PRODUCTION HISTORY

Yellow Flesh / Alabaster Rose had its world premiere at Theatre of NOTE in Los Angeles on February 14, 2003. It was directed by Miguel Montalvo. The scenic design was by Laura Hyman, the costume design was by Kelsey Wedeen, the lighting and sound design was by Robert Oriol, the production stage managers were Lauren Letherer and Dan Wingard, and it was produced by Rosemary Boyce and Joe Foster. The cast was:

ELLIOT	Christopher Neiman
LITTLE B	Alina Phelan
BECKY	Jennifer Ann Evans
ROSE	Rachel Kann
MOM	Sarah Lilly
JUSTIN	Richard Werner
BROOKE/KRISTEN	McKerrin Kelly
MIKE	Ezra Buzzington
JESS STEARN	Scott McKinley
FATHER	Ezra Buzzington

The understudies were: Scott McKinley (Mike), McKerrin Kelly (Becky), Sofie Calderon (Rose), Emily Liu (Brooke), Lauren Letherer (Mom), David Bickford (Jess Stearn), Phinneas Kiyomura (Elliot, Justin), and Kelsey Wedeen (Little B).

CHARACTERS

ELLIOT, a man in his early thirties. Sometimes known as Tom.

LITTLE B, his sister, fifteen.

BECKY, a woman in her early thirties. Sometimes known as Hunter.

ROSE, her daughter, fifteen.

MOM, a mother in her fifties. Named Rose Silverstein.

JUSTIN, a hustler in his late twenties to thirties.

BROOKE/KRISTEN, a phone-sex operator in her twenties to thirties.

MIKE, a hustler in his fifties.

FATHER, a voice/memory (played by the actor who plays Mike).

DR. MARTIN PERKINS, a professor in his fifties.

DR. ALBERT ELLIS, a psychologist in his fifties.

DR. STEARN, a doctor in his fifties.

NOTE: The three doctors should all be played by the same actor.

TIME AND PLACE

It is 2003.

There are many locations. They can be suggested. Don't bother with big set changes. All you really need are a few pieces of furniture and a pole.

PROLOGUE

Two set pieces:

A bed.

And a pole for dancing, at a strip club.

In darkness, we hear the first chords of "It's Oh So Quiet," recorded by Bjork [track #4 on Post*] over the sound system.*

LIGHTS come UP to reveal:

Elliot, Becky, and Little B, each in their own worlds, separate from one another.

Elliot masturbates.

Becky pole dances.

Little B sings along to the recording of Bjork, holding a hairbrush like it's a microphone. Really performing the song: all wide-eyed, whispers and screams.

Both Elliot and Becky's movements should be in tune with the song—gentle when the song is soft, aggressive when the song goes hard.

Somewhere in the middle of the song, Becky stops dancing and leaves the stage.

Just as Little B finishes singing, Elliot orgasms loudly.

BLACKOUT.

ACT ONE

SCENE ONE

Justin gives Elliot head.

Professor Martin Perkins stands away from the action, speaking to the audience. He refers to Elliot and Justin as if they're slides in a presentation. Over-the-top.

PROFESSOR MARTIN PERKINS: Today's homosexual is a
complex, often misunderstood—and therefore maligned—subset
of our current population. Unwilling, or perhaps unable, to
remain in the shadows, the modern homosexual flaunts his wares
wherever he goes. His flagrantly effeminate demeanor, which he
chooses to display through such means as strip shows, drag
brunches, and other recruiting events, is both a cry for help and a
desire for attention. It is no wonder the public at large finds his
behavior so offensive. The modern homosexual wants your
outrage. He craves it!

JUSTIN: Your cum tastes like candy.

ELLIOT: Thanks.

LIGHTS OUT on Elliot and Justin.

3

PROFESSOR MARTIN PERKINS: But it would be a mistake to lump all homosexuals in the same proverbial basket of sin. For while on the outside they appear the same, homosexuals are veritable snowflakes—no two deviants alike in manner. It would be erroneous to judge them as such.

LIGHTS UP on Elliot and Justin.

JUSTIN: Did anyone ever tell you that?
ELLIOT: No.
JUSTIN: I'm gonna fuck you now.
ELLIOT: Okay.
JUSTIN: You want a popper?

LIGHTS OUT on Elliot and Justin.

PROFESSOR MARTIN PERKINS: All their mincing about, their affected manner, their girlish peacocking—at the end of the day, it's not entirely their fault. This pronounced faggotry is a reaction to the way we, as a society, treat them. The homosexual cannot conform to the high standards of intellectual society, so he deforms and denigrates, he contorts and distorts.

In darkness, Elliot moans.

4

PROFESSOR MARTIN PERKINS: The harsh truth is, society has failed the homosexual. And we must reconsider the homosexual's plight if we ever want to reform him.

> *Quick flash of LIGHTS UP on Elliot— bent over at a right angle—Justin fucking him. Then LIGHTS go OUT again.*

PROFESSOR MARTIN PERKINS: It's easy to point fingers at their loathsome behavior.

> *LIGHTS UP on Elliot and Justin kissing. Elliot pushes Justin away from him.*

ELLIOT: Stop.

JUSTIN: What?

ELLIOT: I can't buy you anymore.

JUSTIN: Why not?

ELLIOT: Because I'm beginning to *buy you.*

> *LIGHTS OUT on Elliot and Justin.*

PROFESSOR MARTIN PERKINS: It's easy to pass laws and ban books. But all that does is exacerbate the homosexual problem.

LIGHTS UP on Elliot and Justin, in bed.

There is a KNOCK at the door. (Which Justin does not hear.)

ELLIOT: Who is it?

FATHER'S VOICE: It's your father.

ELLIOT: What do you want?

FATHER'S VOICE: Your mother kicked me out of bed, and someone needs a spanking.

LIGHTS OUT on Elliot.

PROFESSOR MARTIN PERKINS: If we want to truly understand what makes a man a homosexual, we mustn't push him further into the shadows. We must bring him into the light.

LIGHTS UP on Elliot and Justin. Justin and Elliot are making out throughout the rest of this section—undressing, nipple-play, etc.

ELLIOT: I want—

JUSTIN: You want me again?

ELLIOT: Yeah, just—

JUSTIN: What is it?

PROFESSOR MARTIN PERKINS: We must face this issue head-on.

ELLIOT: This is difficult for me to say...

PROFESSOR MARTIN PERKINS: It does no one any good to beat around the bush.

ELLIOT: I'm afraid that you'll—

(*a moan*)

—judge me.

PROFESSOR MARTIN PERKINS: I intend to present you, my unbiased audience, with an impartial look at the comings and goings of this much-maligned subset of our population.

ELLIOT: Do you have any—?

PROFESSOR MARTIN PERKINS: It is not necessary—

ELLIOT: No, let me—

PROFESSOR MARTIN PERKINS: I said, it is not necessary—

ELLIOT: Fantasies.

PROFESSOR MARTIN PERKINS: —for you to agree—

ELLIOT: Do you have any?

PROFESSOR MARTIN PERKINS: —with my findings.

JUSTIN: Like what?

ELLIOT: I want you to—

PROFESSOR MARTIN PERKINS: I present them to you without comment.

ELLIOT: Will you pretend?

PROFESSOR MARTIN PERKINS: Without judgment.

ELLIOT: I want you to—

PROFESSOR MARTIN PERKINS: That's the only way we can understand the preponderance of ponces and puffs in today's otherwise advanced society.

ELLIOT: Will you pretend to be my father?

> *LIGHTS OUT on Elliot and Justin, their eyes locked.*

PROFESSOR MARTIN PERKINS: Now let's get to the heart of the matter.

> *LIGHTS OUT on Professor Martin Perkins.*

> *Lights shift back to Elliot and Justin.*

SCENE TWO

We're in Elliot's bedroom.

Elliot and Justin have just fucked. Elliot is sitting on the edge of his bed, putting his clothes on. Justin lies on the bed, not rushed.

ELLIOT: That was really, really good.
JUSTIN: Good.
ELLIOT: Yeah, thanks.

An awkward moment. Is this it? Are we done? Why isn't Justin getting dressed?

ELLIOT: What's your name?
JUSTIN: Justin.
ELLIOT: Do you want anything to drink? Anything to eat?
JUSTIN: I'm fine.
ELLIOT: I could make cookies.
JUSTIN: Chocolate chip?
ELLIOT: Sure.
JUSTIN: I like chocolate chip.

Elliot exits.

Justin lays there, looks up at the ceiling. A couple of beats, then Elliot comes back with a glass of water and some paper towels. He hands Justin the water.

JUSTIN: Thanks.

ELLIOT: You've got some—

He motions to Justin's stomach.

JUSTIN: Oh.

Elliot wipes the cum off Justin's stomach and out of his belly button.

JUSTIN: Thanks.

Beat.

ELLIOT: Is your name really Justin?

JUSTIN: No.

ELLIOT: What is it?

JUSTIN: Is your name really Tom?

ELLIOT: It's Elliot.

JUSTIN: Elliot.

ELLIOT: What's your real name?

JUSTIN: I don't use it.

ELLIOT: But what is it?

No response.

They stare at each other for a moment.
Elliot waits for a reply. Justin obviously
isn't going to give him one.

ELLIOT: You won't tell me?

JUSTIN: No.

ELLIOT (*annoyed*): I told you mine.

JUSTIN: The world is filled with freaks.

ELLIOT: Fine.

JUSTIN: It's a rule I follow not to use my real name.

ELLIOT: I get it.

JUSTIN: Sorry if that bothers you.

ELLIOT: You get a lot of freaks?

JUSTIN: Yeah.

ELLIOT: What does that mean, exactly?

JUSTIN: Freak?

ELLIOT: How do you define it?

JUSTIN: I don't know.

ELLIOT: Like, do you mean, emotional basket case? Or, like, circus
    carny?

JUSTIN: Emotional basket case.

ELLIOT: Do you think I'm a freak? Is that why you—

JUSTIN: Won't tell you my name?

ELLIOT: Yeah.

JUSTIN: I don't tell any of my clients my name.

ELLIOT: So that's just a—

JUSTIN (*overlapping*): That's just a rule I follow.

ELLIOT: —a rule you follow. Like you said.

JUSTIN: Right.

ELLIOT: Right. Okay, right, anyway, so, are you saying you do or you don't think I'm a freak? You're saying you don't?

JUSTIN: I didn't say that.

ELLIOT: Then you do?

JUSTIN: The jury's still out.

ELLIOT: But which way is the jury leaning?

JUSTIN: Your need to know what I think of you puts you more on the freak side.

ELLIOT: Really? You think curiosity is freakish?

JUSTIN: A certain kind of curiosity.

ELLIOT: I *am* a freak.

JUSTIN: I thought so.

ELLIOT: So you can close the case.

JUSTIN: Emotional or circus?

ELLIOT: I should check on the cookies.

JUSTIN: Okay.

Elliot exits.

Justin picks up a book off the bed stand (some lurid-sounding title—maybe a new book every night). He leafs through it for a moment.

Elliot re-enters.

ELLIOT: Another minute or two.

JUSTIN: Nice book.

ELLIOT: Oh.

JUSTIN: Light reading? Or inspiration?

ELLIOT: It's just a book.

JUSTIN: You mean, mind my own business?

ELLIOT: Do you wanna play a game?

JUSTIN: What kind of game?

ELLIOT: A book game.

JUSTIN: Sure.

ELLIOT: Okay. I'm thinking something in my head. It's a rule. Do you agree to abide by the rule that I have in my head?

JUSTIN: What is it?

ELLIOT: I can't tell you. You have to agree.

JUSTIN: Sure.

ELLIOT: Good. Okay, now. Tell me when to stop.

Elliot flips through pages in the book.

JUSTIN: Stop.

> *Elliot stops. He holds the book open.*

ELLIOT: Tell me when to stop.

> *Elliot alternates between the left page
> and right page.*

JUSTIN: Stop.

> *Elliot stops. He moves his finger up and
> down that page.*

ELLIOT: One more time.
JUSTIN: Stop.

> *Elliot stops.*

ELLIOT: Okay. So. The rule I had in my head was that whatever
　　　sentence you landed on would be our sexual fortune for the rest
　　　of the evening.
JUSTIN: Okay.
ELLIOT: Sometimes it works better than others.
JUSTIN: Read it.
ELLIOT: We might have to interpret.

JUSTIN: Just read it.

Elliot reads whatever sentence his finger has landed on. He should read the entire sentence. If it's a long one, he might first say "It's a long one." The sentence he reads should not be planned. His finger will, presumably, land on a new sentence every night. Feel free to improvise a response. If the sentence Elliot reads doesn't make any sense, the following dialogue could be said:

JUSTIN: That doesn't make sense.
ELLIOT: Sometimes it works better than
    others.
JUSTIN: You warned me.
ELLIOT: This is one of those times that
    didn't work as well I guess.

If the sentence Elliot reads is very sexual, the following dialogue could be said:

JUSTIN: Well.
ELLIOT: So that's our fortune.
JUSTIN: I guess.

15

ELLIOT: For tonight.

JUSTIN: If you say so.

ELLIOT: Yeah.

Have a moment. Say what you want. In any case, the dialogue about the sentence should end with an awkward pause. After a moment:

JUSTIN: Okay, so. Let's get to it.

ELLIOT: Do you smell that?

JUSTIN: What?

ELLIOT: The cookies are burning.

JUSTIN: Forget the cookies. Take your clothes off.

ELLIOT: I have more dough.

JUSTIN: I thought I'd give you the rest of the night for free.

ELLIOT: Cookie dough.

JUSTIN: I know what you meant.

ELLIOT: You're off the clock?

JUSTIN: Yeah.

ELLIOT: You shouldn't do that.

JUSTIN: Why not?

ELLIOT: Because you'll get me.

JUSTIN: I already got you.

ELLIOT: Hooked.

JUSTIN: You'd rather pay?

ELLIOT: I just think it's clever.

JUSTIN: Clever.

ELLIOT: Yeah.

JUSTIN: So.

ELLIOT: Do you—

JUSTIN: Huh?

ELLIOT: Always?

JUSTIN: What?

ELLIOT: Do that?

JUSTIN: If I like them.

ELLIOT: I see.

JUSTIN: Do you?

ELLIOT: I understand.

JUSTIN: And?

ELLIOT: I want it.

JUSTIN: Free?

ELLIOT: Yeah. Just—

JUSTIN: What?

ELLIOT: Make me forget I paid for it the first time.

> *As Elliot goes in for a kiss, LIGHTS OUT.*

SCENE THREE

Elliot kneels over a toilet, puking.

Little B enters.

LITTLE B: Why are you throwing up?

ELLIOT: None of your business.

LITTLE B: "I identify with polar bears."

ELLIOT: Will you shut up?

LITTLE B: "They're very cuddly and cute and quite calm—"

ELLIOT: I'm not in the mood.

LITTLE B: "—but if they meet you, they can be very strong. They come to Iceland very rarely, once every ten years, floating on icebergs."

She looks at Elliot, expectantly.

ELLIOT: Why can't you be normal for once?

LITTLE B: Why are you throwing up?

ELLIOT: I asked you first.

LITTLE B doesn't respond.

ELLIOT: Hand me my toothbrush.

She does. He starts brushing. She takes her brush out and starts brushing too. Mimicking him out of the corner of her eyes. They both spit into the sink.

LITTLE B: Who was he?

ELLIOT: Who was who?

LITTLE B: That man.

ELLIOT: I thought you were asleep.

LITTLE B: No.

ELLIOT: Sorry.

LITTLE B: Can I have a cookie?

ELLIOT: Sure.

LITTLE B: The ones you made are burnt.

ELLIOT: When mom comes by tomorrow, don't tell her there was a man here.

LITTLE B: Will you make some cookies that aren't burnt?

ELLIOT: And don't tell her I threw up.

LITTLE B: Will you?

ELLIOT: What are you telling mom?

LITTLE B: There was no man, you didn't throw up.

ELLIOT: Okay, I'll make you cookies.

LITTLE B: Chocolate chip?

ELLIOT: You know you're gonna have to brush your teeth again?

Little B nods.

ELLIOT: Chocolate chip.

Lights shift.

SCENE FOUR

Elliot's on the phone.

Separately, Brooke is curled up on a couch, multitasking (maybe she's knitting?) while she talks on the phone.

ELLIOT: What are you wearing?

BROOKE: Nothing. I'm naked.

ELLIOT: Really? That's jumping the gun a little, don't you think?

BROOKE: What?

ELLIOT: Why don't you put something on so we can talk about how it's coming off?

BROOKE: Okay, I'm wearing clothes.

ELLIOT: What?

BROOKE: I've got clothes on.

ELLIOT: What?

BROOKE: I said, "I've got clothes on."

ELLIOT: You think you can just say, "Okay, I've got clothes on," and I'll believe you?

BROOKE: Yes.

ELLIOT: You said you were naked just seconds ago, to already be dressed defies logic.

BROOKE: I'm not selling you logic. I'm selling you the idea of my naked body.

ELLIOT: I understand that. I understand that. And I also understand that we're separated by a phone line, so you can say whatever you want. I mean, we probably don't even live in the same state.

BROOKE: I live in California.

ELLIOT: Really?

BROOKE: Where'd you see my ad?

ELLIOT: LA Weekly.

BROOKE: I live in Silverlake.

ELLIOT: I didn't think that necessarily meant—

BROOKE: Where do you live?

ELLIOT: Hollywood.

BROOKE: We're neighbors. I'm Brooke.

ELLIOT: Well, okay, Brooke, um, what I'm trying to say is that if I'm going to get off, then we have to be complicit in this.

BROOKE: All right?

ELLIOT: So you really have to do your part too.

BROOKE: Are you trying to tell me how to do my job?

ELLIOT: I'm just saying that you can't get away with saying one thing one second and then another thing the next second because then I'm really gonna think you're lying to me.

BROOKE (*getting emotional*): Maybe you should just call back.

ELLIOT: No—

BROOKE: Talk to another girl.

ELLIOT: We can talk, that's fine.

BROOKE: They told me I'd have to deal with creeps, but I didn't—

ELLIOT: What?

BROOKE: I thought today—

ELLIOT: What did you think?

BROOKE: I didn't really think it would be that hard to do.

ELLIOT: What are you talking about?

BROOKE: This is my first day...

ELLIOT: Your first...?

BROOKE: I mean, how hard can it be?

ELLIOT: I didn't realize it was your first day.

BROOKE: Just be sexy right?

ELLIOT: I'm sorry.

BROOKE: That's all I have to do.

ELLIOT: I didn't mean to be a creep.

BROOKE: Be sexy.

ELLIOT: Right.

BROOKE: That's not supposed to be hard.

ELLIOT: You have a sexy voice.

BROOKE: Really?

ELLIOT: I've been meaning to say something. It's very sexy.

BROOKE: You're not just saying?

ELLIOT: No.

BROOKE: Because you don't have to lie to me. I can take it. I guess I
    need to know what I'm doing wrong so I don't keep fucking up.

ELLIOT: I feel really bad that I gave you a lecture.

BROOKE: No, really, it's fine.

ELLIOT: But that's not really like me.

BROOKE: It's okay.

ELLIOT: It's just that I get into moods sometimes and I'm kind of in one right now.

BROOKE: Why?

ELLIOT: I'm just having a bad day.

BROOKE: What happened?

ELLIOT: Nothing.

BROOKE: Are you okay?

ELLIOT: I'm okay, I don't really know.

BROOKE: Your voice is sexy too.

ELLIOT: Thanks.

BROOKE: You're welcome.

ELLIOT: You're really sweet.

BROOKE: Thanks.

ELLIOT: So I was in this mood and that's why I called you, I thought it would get me out of this funk that I'm in, at least for a minute or two, 'cause I feel good when I'm jerking off, and that's something that I can't deny...

BROOKE: You don't sound like a creep anymore.

ELLIOT: Really?

BROOKE: I can definitely imagine kissing you...fucking you...

ELLIOT: See, you can do this!

BROOKE: It helps to warm into things.

ELLIOT: I don't think that everyone could do it.

BROOKE: It's just talking. Everyone can do that.

ELLIOT: Not everyone.

BROOKE: Maybe not mutes.

ELLIOT: Listen, we've gotten off subject. I have an idea—why don't we start at the beginning again?

BROOKE: Okay.

ELLIOT: Okay, and I want to start where you tried to start things, where I messed up and judged you.

BROOKE: When was that?

ELLIOT: When you first said you were naked.

BROOKE: Oh, right.

ELLIOT: Yes, right, so you're already naked. Now. I want you to get dressed and I want you to describe every step of the way.

BROOKE: Backwards?

ELLIOT: Yeah, we'll get dressed first and *then* we'll take things off again. It'll be that much more exciting.

BROOKE: Okay. So I'm naked.

ELLIOT: Good.

BROOKE: Now I'm putting on my top.

ELLIOT: Your top first? That's backwards.

BROOKE: Doggy-style.

ELLIOT: Doggy, doggy, doggy, yeah, that's sexy, that's good. And no bra?

BROOKE: No bra.

ELLIOT: That's a good image, I like it.

BROOKE: The naked lower half of my body...

ELLIOT: Yeah...

BROOKE: The naked lower half of my body is cold and I'm getting all goose-pimply.

ELLIOT: That's good. Um. I'm sorry, could you, um, I have call
      waiting, I'll just be a second.
BROOKE: Okay.

He clicks over.

ELLIOT: Hello?...Hi, I'm, um, busy right now, could you...could I
      call you back?...What is it? She's fine...That was just a dream, I
      promise you she's fine, go back to sleep...Look, I've got
      someone on hold and it's an expensive call...I know it's
      late...yes, it's long distance...Look, I'll call you back
      tomorrow...Okay, you too, bye.

He clicks back.

      Hey, are you still there?
BROOKE: Yes.
ELLIOT: Where were we? I got distracted, I forget where we were.
BROOKE: I'm wearing my blouse and nothing else.
ELLIOT: Right, that's right, you're wearing your blouse and nothing
      else. That's hot. Describe your blouse to me.
BROOKE: Well, to start off, it's made of rayon.
ELLIOT: Really? Rayon?
BROOKE: Yes.
ELLIOT: I'm having a difficult time imagining that.
BROOKE: It's a kind of artificial silk.

ELLIOT: Does it feel like silk?

BROOKE: Kind of.

ELLIOT: Well, it sounds weird to me. Could you—

BROOKE: Rayon?

ELLIOT: Yes, rayon. Rough and un-sexy. Could we—

BROOKE: What?

ELLIOT: Could we say it's cotton and white and your nipples are
poking through the material?

BROOKE: It's cotton and white and my nipples are poking through the
material.

ELLIOT: Okay, good, I like when you say that.

BROOKE: It's cotton and white and my nipples are poking through the
material.

ELLIOT: Tell me more about your nipples.

BROOKE: My areola are the size of the rim of a beer can.

ELLIOT: Yeah? That's hot. Say that again. "Areola."

BROOKE: Areola.

ELLIOT: That's hot. Your nipples are hot. You have hot nipples.
Could you—*fuck*—I'm sorry, hold on one second, just a second,
I'm sorry.

He clicks over.

Hello?...Why are you calling me again?...Do we have to do this
right now? I really don't want to have this conversation...Well,
they're not the same person, all right? Little B isn't going to run

27

away...I'm sorry, I didn't mean to be...yes, I'm sorry, I said I was sorry, I'm sorry...I was going to, I would have...I'm still on long distance...yeah, yes, I am...I know, it's a long call and it's costing me a lot of money right now to be talking to you...I don't know how much...Two-ninety-five a minute or something ridiculous like that...yeah, yeah, I know, I need a new long distance carrier, I'm going to get right on that, I will, GOODNIGHT...Good-bye.

He clicks back.

Hello, hey, are you still there?

BROOKE: Of course I am.

ELLIOT: It wouldn't be in your best interest to hang up, would it?

BROOKE: No.

ELLIOT: Right, okay, anyway, I'm tired of this clothes talk, let's just say we're both naked. Now what?

BROOKE: I'm sitting on my bed and I'm fondling my breasts.

ELLIOT: I'm sorry, wait, hold that thought, that's good, I can imagine where it's going and it's good, I don't mean to interrupt, but...

BROOKE: You'll just be a second?

ELLIOT: Yes, yes, I'll just be a second.

He clicks over.

What do you want?...I did just check on her, she's fine, she's in

28

bed...No, no, you can't talk to her...Because she's sleeping. I'll have her call you in the morning...I know. I know you don't see her enough, but that's not my fault, is it?...No, I'm not blaming you. Listen, why don't you come over tomorrow morning and have breakfast with her? How's that?...Okay, good...Okay, go to sleep. Bye.

He clicks back.

She's going to drive me crazy.

BROOKE: Your girlfriend?

ELLIOT: My mother. She's—I'm sorry, I really don't want to talk about her, you were fondling your breasts, can we take it from there?

The phone clicks. On Elliot's exasperated sigh, we BLACKOUT.

SCENE FIVE

Little B is in her room, singing "Hyperballad" [Track #2 from Bjork's album Post*].*

Separately, Elliot is in his room, sitting on the edge of his bed, his pants around his ankles. Brooke is giving him a blowjob. He cums.

She stumbles out of the room. We hear her spit, cough, gag, spit.

She re-enters.

[Note: They have to yell over the Bjork music to be heard.]

BROOKE: You've got a lot of, you know...
ELLIOT: Cum?
BROOKE: Yeah.
ELLIOT: I know.
BROOKE: When was the last time you...
ELLIOT: Came?
BROOKE: Yeah.

ELLIOT: This morning.

BROOKE: No.

ELLIOT: You don't believe me?

BROOKE: I've just never seen a guy...

ELLIOT: Cum so much?

BROOKE: Yeah.

ELLIOT: Oh.

BROOKE: What did you have for lunch?

ELLIOT: Why?

BROOKE: Your, you know—

ELLIOT: Cum.

BROOKE: Was kind of bitter.

ELLIOT: Really?

BROOKE: Yeah.

ELLIOT: Sorry.

BROOKE: It's okay.

ELLIOT: McDonald's.

BROOKE: Really?

ELLIOT: Yeah.

BROOKE: That's strange.

ELLIOT: Why?

BROOKE: You'd think fast food would make it taste better.

ELLIOT: You would?

BROOKE: The grease and all.

ELLIOT: I thought prostitutes weren't supposed to complain.

BROOKE: I'm not complaining, I'm just saying.

ELLIOT: You said my cum tasted bad.

BROOKE: Not bad, just bitter.

ELLIOT: So it was just an observation?

BROOKE: Yes.

ELLIOT: Can we agree that I'm paying for the privilege of sex without observations?

BROOKE: If that's what you want?

ELLIOT: I don't mean to be rude.

BROOKE: I have no comment.

Beat.

See—I can refrain from observation.

ELLIOT: Good.

BROOKE: This isn't an observation, this is a question: Who's the girl?

ELLIOT: I'm sorry, is she—

BROOKE: Bothering me?

ELLIOT: Yeah.

BROOKE: No. Just, who is she?

ELLIOT: She's my sister.

BROOKE: I figured she wasn't your girlfriend.

ELLIOT: No.

BROOKE: But you never know.

ELLIOT: What's that supposed to mean?

BROOKE: I mean, I figure some girlfriends are probably more lenient about things like this. I didn't mean to imply anything about your sister.

ELLIOT: I didn't infer anything unseemly.

BROOKE: Your sister likes to sing.

ELLIOT: Yeah.

BROOKE: She sings a lot.

ELLIOT: Yeah.

BROOKE: Does she take requests?

ELLIOT: Is that a joke?

BROOKE: Maybe.

ELLIOT: No.

BROOKE: Is she practicing for something?

ELLIOT: Like a recital?

BROOKE: Sure.

ELLIOT: No.

BROOKE: She just likes to sing?

ELLIOT: Yes.

BROOKE: Do you not like me or something?

ELLIOT: Why do you say that?

BROOKE: Because you became distant all of a sudden.

ELLIOT: I like you.

BROOKE: What are you thinking?

ELLIOT: Nothing.

BROOKE: I can see in your eyes that you're thinking something.

He doesn't say anything. They look at each other for a count of 60. This will hopefully time out to coincide with the end of 'Hyperballad.'

ELLIOT: I'm not thinking anything.

BLACKOUT.

SCENE SIX

*Elliot's bedroom. Elliot enters with Mike,
a hustler.*

ELLIOT: This is my room.

MIKE: Nice room, Tom.

ELLIOT: Are you being sarcastic?

MIKE: No.

ELLIOT: It's just that—I'm sorry, what was your name again?

MIKE: Mike.

ELLIOT: That's right, anyway, thanks for coming over. Sorry it's so
    late.

MIKE: The ad says 24/7.

ELLIOT: I was just making small talk.

> *Elliot awkwardly goes in for a kiss, but
> before he can reach Mike's lips:*

MIKE: I get paid up front.

ELLIOT: Right.

> *Elliot gets his wallet, pays Mike. Mike
> begins to undress.*

ELLIOT: Slow down. Not just yet.

MIKE: All right.

ELLIOT: You want anything to drink?

MIKE: I'm fine.

ELLIOT: Party?

MIKE: No thanks.

ELLIOT: I don't usually, it's just been a long day.

MIKE: I don't need an explanation.

> *Elliot takes out a small vial of coke,*
> *snorts a line.*

MIKE: Now why don't you give your daddy a kiss?

ELLIOT: What did you say?

MIKE: Give your daddy a kiss.

> *Elliot goes to him, kisses him. For*
> *several beats. Stops. Pulls away.*

ELLIOT: How did you know I—

MIKE: That's what you like, right?

ELLIOT: Yes.

MIKE: That's what you want, right?

ELLIOT: Yes.

MIKE: Then let's do this right. Get in bed.

ELLIOT: Yes, sir.

Mike watches Elliot get into bed. Then he leaves.

There is a KNOCK at the door.

ELLIOT: Who is it?

MIKE (*from off-stage*): It's your father.

ELLIOT: What do you want?

MIKE (*from off-stage*): Your mother kicked me out of bed, and someone needs a spanking.

ELLIOT: Come in.

Mike enters.

ELLIOT: Dad, what are you doing here?

MIKE: I thought I'd check on you.

ELLIOT: But why aren't you with mom?

MIKE: Your mother has a headache.

ELLIOT: She kicked you out of bed?

MIKE: Yes.

ELLIOT: I'm sorry.

MIKE: Can I sleep in here, son?

ELLIOT: Yes.

As Mike gets into the bed, BLACKOUT.

SCENE SEVEN

Elliot is alone on stage. Talking to himself, practicing a conversation.

ELLIOT: Hi. Hello. Hi.

 This is—

 This is—

 It's me, it's Tom.

 I am so—.

 Hi, my name's Tom and I enjoy sunny days, long walks on the beach, and, um...

 Fuck me. No, really.

 Hi, I'm Tom, what's your—

 I'm a Leo.

 No, I don't believe in—

 No, I don't.

 Oh, really, you're a Leo Rising?

 I don't know what that means.

 I mean, I don't believe in any of that destiny nonsense.

 Okay, wait, start over.

 Hi, I'm Tom. Tim? Timmy? Tom-Tom. I'm Tom.

 Nice to—. Yes I'd like a lapdance.

 How long have you—?

 Oh, you don't fuck?

 No, that's fine, I wasn't even—

I mean, I didn't—

That's not what I—

No, that's okay, you can just dance.

Really.

That's an interesting stage name.

Okay, wait, start over.

Do you want a drink?

I need to get a buzz on.

Are you already loaded?

I need to get fucking loaded.

You have really nice lips.

I mean it.

They're unbelievably persuasive.

I want you.

I do.

Okay, listen, you can call me Elliot.

Really?

You think I have yellow skin?

That's funny, I was born with jaundice but right now I think it's just the light.

BLACKOUT.

SCENE EIGHT

At a STRIP CLUB. A small cubicle.
Becky enters first, followed by Elliot.

BECKY: Have a seat.
ELLIOT: Okay.

He sits.

Hi.
BECKY: Hi.
ELLIOT: Hi.
BECKY: Hello.
ELLIOT: Um. What's your name?
BECKY: Hunter.
ELLIOT: Really?
BECKY: Sure. What's yours?
ELLIOT: Tom.
BECKY: Glad we got that out of the way, Tom.
ELLIOT: What do you—um...
BECKY: What?
ELLIOT: What?
BECKY: You've got a mouth.
ELLIOT: What's that mean?
BECKY: You can speak, can't you?

ELLIOT: Yeah.

BECKY: Then say what you want to say.

ELLIOT: I've never had a lap dance before. I'm not sure what the
parameters are. I wasn't really expecting to talk.

BECKY: What were you expecting?

ELLIOT: I thought you'd be dancing by now.

BECKY: I can dance.

ELLIOT: Okay.

BECKY: If that's all you want.

ELLIOT: You do more?

BECKY: That depends.

ELLIOT: On what?

BECKY: On you. On money. On things.

ELLIOT: For now, I'd like a lap dance.

BECKY: Then let's hit it.

*She snaps her fingers. Some sexy-groovy-
base beats begin to pump through the
sound system. Becky sways her hips.*

BLACKOUT.

SCENE NINE

Elliot's bedroom. Elliot and Justin have just fucked.

JUSTIN: So how was it?

ELLIOT: Good.

JUSTIN: That's all you're gonna say?

ELLIOT: You were great.

JUSTIN: Do you like me better when I give it to you free or when you pay me?

ELLIOT: What kind of question is that?

JUSTIN: Just a question.

ELLIOT: It's always good.

JUSTIN: Good...You wanna go at it again?

ELLIOT: I don't know.

JUSTIN: I think you want to.

ELLIOT: I'm fine. I'm tired.

Justin grabs one of Elliot's nipples and pinches hard. Elliot slaps his hand away.

ELLIOT: Stop.

JUSTIN: So you're done tonight?

ELLIOT: I guess so.

JUSTIN: No cookies?

ELLIOT: You want cookies?

JUSTIN: What are you doing tomorrow?

ELLIOT: Working.

JUSTIN: Tomorrow at 7 p.m.?

ELLIOT: Home schooling my sister.

JUSTIN: Because I was thinking we could get together for dinner or something.

ELLIOT: Are you inviting me or are you inviting yourself?

JUSTIN: Actually, I think you said something about dinner last week. You said, 'We see so much of each other in here, it's time we see some of each other out there'—that's what you said.

ELLIOT: Do you have a tape recorder up your ass or something?

JUSTIN: Just my head.

ELLIOT: You have your head up your ass?

JUSTIN: That's not what I meant.

ELLIOT: Look, I can't afford this anymore.

JUSTIN: You can't?

ELLIOT: No.

JUSTIN: And that's why you've been so cold?

ELLIOT: Yes.

JUSTIN: That's funny.

ELLIOT: What is?

JUSTIN: Nothing. You can't afford me.

ELLIOT: Do you even know what I do for a living?

JUSTIN: You've never told me.

ELLIOT: I teach high school. I teach remedial English to kids who've made it this far without learning how to read.

JUSTIN: Would you go out to dinner with me if my name was Mike?

ELLIOT: Are you even listening to me?

JUSTIN: You can afford to fuck Mike.

ELLIOT: How do you know about Mike?

JUSTIN: He's my tell. I tell him where I'm going before I leave for outcalls. He tells me where he's going. We tell each other everything.

ELLIOT: No, I can't afford Mike either.

JUSTIN: So that was just a one-time thing?

ELLIOT: I don't think I really have to explain myself to you.

JUSTIN: The ironic thing is that I was going to start giving it to you for free all of the time. You're my favorite client.

ELLIOT: Still a client.

JUSTIN: But that's been changing. Didn't you feel it?

ELLIOT: Is this twenty questions? I said I don't want it.

JUSTIN: So you're not gonna buy it from anyone anymore? Not me? Not Mike?

ELLIOT: No.

JUSTIN: Is there someone else?

ELLIOT: Yes.

JUSTIN: You have a boyfriend.

ELLIOT: Something like that.

JUSTIN: What's his name?

ELLIOT: *Her* name's Brooke.

JUSTIN: She's a girl?

ELLIOT: Yeah.

JUSTIN: A girl girl?

ELLIOT: Yes.

JUSTIN: How old is she?

ELLIOT: I don't want to talk about her.

JUSTIN: Come on. Give me some details.

ELLIOT: I don't know. Late 20's?

JUSTIN: Do you fuck her in the ass or in her vagina?

ELLIOT: This is sick.

JUSTIN: Come on.

ELLIOT: I can't talk about this with you.

JUSTIN: I think you're paying for him.

ELLIOT: Who?

JUSTIN: "Brooke."

ELLIOT: "Her."

JUSTIN: It all sounds so wonderful.

ELLIOT: It is.

JUSTIN: Really?

ELLIOT: That's one of my verbal tics. I say it a lot. "Really?" I think
    I'm rubbing off on you.

JUSTIN: I just don't see you as the type who plays for both teams.

ELLIOT: I hate that.

JUSTIN: You seem more fag to me.

ELLIOT: When people say things like that they sound like fucking
    idiots.

JUSTIN: I think you're pushing me away because you're falling in love with me and that's too much for you to bear.

ELLIOT: Hardly.

JUSTIN: My real name is Robert, but my parents are the only people who ever called me that. Mom's dead; dad's got a restaurant in Tucson. My friends and lovers all call me Bobby. I'm ready to tell you more. I'm ready to let you in. But you're gonna have to start paying again to win back my trust.

ELLIOT: Stop.

JUSTIN: You know that scar on the inner part of my right thigh?

ELLIOT: Stop it.

JUSTIN: I used to have a tattoo that said 'Michael' but I removed it.

ELLIOT: I don't care.

JUSTIN: I love you. I want to let you in.

ELLIOT: No you don't.

JUSTIN: I do. I've been falling in love with you.

ELLIOT: I erased your number from my cell phone.

JUSTIN: Don't you know it by heart?

ELLIOT: I'm not gonna call you again.

JUSTIN: Three-two-three, six-six-two—

ELLIOT: —LEAVE—

JUSTIN: —eight-five-four-nine.

ELLIOT: Now.

JUSTIN: No.

ELLIOT: What?

JUSTIN: You haven't paid for me yet.

ELLIOT: You said it was a freebie.

JUSTIN: It was a freebie when I thought we had something.

ELLIOT: I don't have any money.

JUSTIN: I don't give freebies to people who don't love me. I know you've got cash.

> *Elliot grabs his wallet. He hands Justin two twenty-dollar bills.*

ELLIOT: That's all I have.

JUSTIN: You're the worst fucking liar I've ever met.

> *Elliot hands him two more twenties.*

JUSTIN: Now *that's* all you have. I know because I counted while you were in the bathroom.

ELLIOT: Will you go now?

> *The phone rings once. They both look at it. It rings again.*

JUSTIN: Aren't you going to answer it?

> *The phone rings a third time, Elliot picks it up.*

ELLIOT (*into phone*): Hello? What's wrong?...No, no, she's
    fine...I'm sure. I put her to bed a few hours ago...What kind of
    dream?...Uh-huh. Okay. That was just a nightmare. She's
    fine...No, mom, Little B isn't going anywhere. I promise you, I
    won't let that happen. Go back to sleep...You can't sleep? Yes
    you can...I will, I will, I'll go check on her right now and let you
    know that she's breathing. Then you'll go to sleep? Okay, good,
    hold on.

(*to Justin*)

Do you mind leaving? I have to take care of something.
JUSTIN: I can tell that you're a good son.
ELLIOT: How many times do I have to tell you to leave before you're
    going to listen to me?
JUSTIN: When you start missing me, don't hesitate to give your daddy
    a call.
ELLIOT: I won't.
JUSTIN: You won't hesitate?
ELLIOT: I won't miss you. I won't call.
JUSTIN: One last kiss?
ELLIOT: My mom's on hold. This really isn't the time.
JUSTIN: One last kiss for Daddy?

BLACKOUT.

SCENE TEN

A deep base beat pumps through the sound system. Elliot is sitting in a large overstuffed red loveseat. Becky stands over him, swaying her hips to the beat of the bump.

She rides his knee. Thumping and pumping and blow-your-house-down-ing.

She unbuttons her blouse, takes it off, revealing two butterfly pasties. She rubs her hands through Elliot's hair, pushes his head into her bosom.

ELLIOT: Stop.

BECKY: What?

ELLIOT: This is too weird.

BLACKOUT.

SCENE ELEVEN

Little B in bed. She starts moaning, soft at first, then louder.

LITTLE B: Get off me. Get off me...

She starts screaming—a deep, emotional wailing/koning. Elliot enters.

ELLIOT: Little B!

He grabs her. She kicks and screams, trying to get out of his arms.

LITTLE B: GetoffmegetoffmeGETOFFME!
ELLIOT: It's okay, it's okay, wake up, Elliot's here, wake up.
LITTLE B: I can't see you!
ELLIOT: It's okay, calm down, I'm right here.
LITTLE B: I hear you but I can't see you! Get off me!

She hits his face, trying to fight him off.

LITTLE B: Get off me!
ELLIOT: Little B! Little B! Listen to me! It's Elliot!
LITTLE B: Where are you, Elliot? I can't find you!

50

ELLIOT: You're not awake. Wake up, I'm here, it's Elliot, I love you.

LITTLE B: I can hear you, Elliot, but I can't see you. Make him stop, stop, stop, stop, stop, stop...

ELLIOT: You're burning up.   LITTLE B: ...stop, stop, stop...

Elliot runs off to the bathroom.   LITTLE B: stopstopstop STOP.

ELLIOT (*from off*): It's okay B! I'm right here! I'm getting you water. I love you Little B! It's okay! [*etc.*]

                              Elliot returns with a wet washcloth. He grabs Little B and holds her and wets her face and hugs her and soothes her.

ELLIOT: ...it's okay, it's okay...   LITTLE B:...stop, stop, stop...

                              She slowly stops fighting and looks at him. One of her legs is intensely shaking.

LITTLE B: Were you just sitting on my bed stand?

ELLIOT: No, it's okay, wake up.

LITTLE B: Elliot?

(*crying*)

I love you, I love you, I love you.

ELLIOT: I love you too. Are you awake?

LITTLE B: I don't know.

ELLIOT: It's okay. You're shaking. Try to stop shaking.

LITTLE B: I can't.

ELLIOT: It's okay. I'm right here. Can you see me?

LITTLE B: I'm trying to find you.

ELLIOT: I'm right here.

LITTLE B: I'm so afraid. It's scary. Make him stop.

ELLIOT: Look at me. He's gone. There's nothing but me, your
brother, Elliot, I love you, do you see me?

LITTLE B: I think so.

ELLIOT: It's me.

LITTLE B: Is that really you?

ELLIOT: Let me check.

He looks at himself.

Yeah, it's me.

She hugs him tight.

ELLIOT: I love you, Little B. You're gonna be all right.

LITTLE B: I don't know where I am.

ELLIOT: This is your room.

LITTLE B: I want mom.

ELLIOT: I know, but she lives at her house, so you can't have her right now, remember?

Little B nods.

ELLIOT: I'll go pick her up tomorrow afternoon and bring her here and you can see her then, okay.

LITTLE B: I want her now.

ELLIOT: Please tell me one other thing that you want right now that maybe I can do.

LITTLE B: I want you to sing to me.

ELLIOT: Okay, good. I can do that. What do you want me to sing?

LITTLE B: Track number four.

ELLIOT: "It's Oh So Quiet"?

LITTLE B: Yes.

ELLIOT: Okay.

(*singing*)

"Shhh, shhh. It's oh so quiet, shhh, shhh, it's oh so still, shhh, shhh..." [etc.]

He rocks her in his arms, she slowly regains composure, she sings along with her brother occasionally, almost under her breath.

LIGHTS OUT.

ACT TWO

SCENE ONE

Dr. Albert Ellis enters.

ALBERT ELLIS, Ph.D.: "Now. I present to you a woman who in our society would commonly be called a 'nymphomaniac.' Although her case is frankly fictionalized, it is based on actual psychiatric histories, which I have culled from a large number of clinical records to which I have had access."

> *In darkness, we hear "This Is Hardcore" by Pulp. The lights slowly come up to reveal: Becky on the floor, masturbating. A knock at the door.*

BECKY: Who is it?
FATHER'S VOICE: It's dad.

> *MUSIC CUTS OUT/BLACKOUT.*

> *LIGHTS UP ON: Dr. Albert Ellis. He talks directly to the audience.*

ALBERT ELLIS, Ph.D.: "Not only is my portrait authentic, but it tends to be a fairly typical representation of many compulsively promiscuous women."

BLACKOUT.

"This is Hardcore" begins playing again, from the top. The lights slowly come up to reveal Becky dancing at a pole. There is a knock at the door.

BECKY: Who's there?

FATHER'S VOICE: Sweetness?

BECKY: What do you want?

FATHER'S VOICE: Your mother has a headache.

MUSIC CUTS OUT/BLACKOUT.

LIGHTS UP ON Dr. Ellis.

ALBERT ELLIS, Ph.D.: "For one thing, it is notable that the female in this study is not a truly hypersexed creature, often fantasized by wishful-thinking males. This male-inspired portrait of a nymphomaniac is largely sheer myth. The majority of 'oversexed' females are really driven to promiscuity, and sometimes to outright prostitution, not by a surplus of hormones

56

or by specific sexual urges, but by various nonsexual or quasi-sexual impulsions—especially the dire need to be loved and approved by their partners."

Again, the same song begins playing, from the top. LOUDER. Lights slowly come up to reveal Becky pole dancing.

There is a knock at the door. Becky looks at the door. Doesn't say anything.

The music stops and starts from the top. Becky goes back to the top of her dance. Begins dancing again.

Each time the music restarts, Becky tries to begin her pole dance anew. This becomes more and more difficult. She tries not to focus her gaze on the door, tries not to think of who stands behind it, but she can't help it. She grows more and more awkward. Physically, her body language regresses from that of a confidant and mature woman to that of an awkward adolescent. Disjointed.

57

ALBERT ELLIS, Ph.D.: "For every nymphomaniac who longs for the sensuous intertwining of her body with nearly every man, there are five or ten other highly promiscuous women who keep bed-hopping in spite of the fact that they are not really overenthusiastic about sex itself, and in spite of the fact that some of them are actually frigid and rarely or never receive orgasmic release. This is not to say that *all* nymphomaniacs are sexually cold, non-orgasmic, or inclined toward lesbianism. A surprisingly large number of them are. However, in my psychotherapy practice, I have seen several compulsively promiscuous women who truly were highly sexed, and who had no difficulty whatever in achieving explosive sexual climaxes in a variety of ways, including regular intercourse. Some of these women, in fact, could have multiple orgasms—as many as ten or twenty a night—practically every day of the year.

> *The music restarts. Becky goes back to the top.*

Nonetheless, they were nymphomaniacs rather than healthfully high-sexed women, not because of their frequent heterosexual adventures, but largely because they engaged in these adventures on an obsessive-compulsive, driven basis instead of in a fully preferential, strongly desirous (rather than direly needful) manner. For compulsivity is the true distinguishing character of the female who is correctly called a 'nymphomaniac.'"

There is another knock at the door.

BECKY: I'm not here.

FATHER'S VOICE: Can I come in?

> *The music restarts. Becky goes back to the top.*

ALBERT ELLIS, Ph.D.: "Nymphomaniacs do not even have to be exceptionally indiscriminate or unselective in their sex activities."

BECKY: I'm asleep.

FATHER'S VOICE: Unlock your door, Becky.

> *The music restarts. Becky goes back to the top.*

ALBERT ELLIS, Ph.D.: "The woman in this case study has been utterly *driven* to her lovers' arms; and it is this sick quality, this propensity to engage in and maintain a sex relationship with a man *at all costs*, even to the physical and emotional detriment of the woman who thereby participates, that is the true hallmark of nymphomania."

BECKY: What do you want?

FATHER'S VOICE: I want to tell you how proud you make me.

The music restarts. Becky goes back to the top.

ALBERT ELLIS, Ph.D.: "Occasionally, as in the case of endogenous nymphomania, the compulsive drive that forces a woman to have sex relations with several (and sometimes an incredibly large number of) men is physiologically based—"

The music restarts. Becky goes back to the top.

"—and results from some hormonal or brain disorder of a serious nature."

BECKY: I want you to go away.

The music restarts. Becky goes back to the top.

ALBERT ELLIS, Ph.D.: "But in the great majority of instances—"

FATHER'S VOICE: When someone pays you a compliment, you ought to reciprocate.

The music restarts. Becky goes back to the top.

ALBERT ELLIS, Ph.D.: "—compulsive promiscuity in the female seems to be psychologically motivated—"

BECKY: Please go away.

The music restarts. Becky goes back to the top.

ALBERT ELLIS, Ph.D.: "—and springs from highly irrational ideas about herself and the world—"

FATHER'S VOICE: Please what?

The music restarts. Becky goes back to the top.

ALBERT ELLIS, Ph.D.: "—ideas that the nymphomaniac acquires—"

BECKY: Pretty please?

ALBERT ELLIS, Ph.D.: "—and nurtures—"

FATHER'S VOICE: That's better.

ALBERT ELLIS, Ph.D.: "—from her early life—"

FATHER'S VOICE: Now just open the door.

ALBERT ELLIS, Ph.D.: "—to, sometimes,—"

FATHER'S VOICE: And give me a goodnight kiss.

ALBERT ELLIS, Ph.D.: "—her very—"

FATHER'S VOICE: And I will forgive you.

ALBERT ELLIS, Ph.D.: "—old age."

FATHER'S VOICE: And everything will be all right.

The music comes to a full stop.

Becky walks to the door to let him in.

ALBERT ELLIS, Ph.D.: Now let's get to the heart of the matter.

BLACKOUT.

SCENE TWO

A kitchen. Strikingly normal.

Rose, Becky's teenage daughter, sits at the kitchen table, reading a book.

BECKY: Is that your homework?
ROSE: No.
BECKY: What is it?
ROSE: A book.
BECKY: What's it called?

Rose hands her the book ("Go Ask Alice"). Becky looks it over, hands it back to her. Rose goes back to her reading.

BECKY: Do you like it? Is it good?

No response.

BECKY: I cut my hair. Do you like it?

Rose looks at her like she's crazy.

BECKY: Can you tell? I only had them take off a few inches.

Rose continues to read, ignoring her mother.

BECKY: What are you doing tonight?

No response.

BECKY: Rose.

ROSE: What?

BECKY: What are you doing tonight?

ROSE: Going to Jenny's house.

BECKY: Sleepover?

ROSE: Yes.

BECKY: Why don't you invite Jenny over here?

ROSE: Why?

BECKY: You slept at her place last weekend.

ROSE: So?

BECKY: We should reciprocate.

ROSE: What's that mean?

BECKY: It means you don't take advantage of your friend's hospitality.

ROSE: What do you care?

BECKY: I'm trying to teach you how to be an adult.

ROSE: I'm not five.

BECKY: I'll take you both out for Chinese before I go to work. I'll rent you some movies. You'll have the house to yourself. You won't have to listen to me.

ROSE: Are you on crack?

BECKY: Rose, I need to say something. I wasn't sure how to say it, but I'm just going to. To get it out in the air.

ROSE: What?

BECKY: I have to ask you a question.

ROSE: Then ask it.

BECKY: Do you know what a blowjob is?

ROSE: WHAT?

BECKY: You do know what a blowjob is, right?

ROSE: Oh my god.

BECKY: Do you?

ROSE: I'm fifteen, mom, not a fucking idiot.

BECKY: So you do?

ROSE: Yes.

BECKY: What is it?

ROSE: Are you serious?

BECKY: Yes.

ROSE: Fuck.

BECKY: No. No. You can say "shit." You can say "shit" all you want. But you can't say fuck until you're eighteen.

ROSE: Like you would even know when that was.

BECKY: I want to know what you know. What's a blowjob?

ROSE: Seriously?

BECKY: You're not going to Jenny's until you tell me what a blowjob
    is.

ROSE: It's when you suck a guy's dick.

BECKY: Right.

ROSE: Are you happy?

BECKY: Have you been to one of those parties?

ROSE: What parties?

BECKY: I talked to Allison Hecker's mom.

ROSE: Why?

BECKY: Allison told her about the party at Carrie's house.

ROSE: What is this—why are you—

BECKY: Were you there?

ROSE: Which Carrie?

BECKY: You went to elementary school with her. Carrie Turner.

ROSE: So?

BECKY: Did you go to her party?

ROSE: No.

BECKY: You didn't go to Carrie's party?

ROSE: I said no.

BECKY: Carrie's mom got home early.

ROSE: I'm going outside—

BECKY: Stay there. Carrie's mom walked in on them.

ROSE: I wasn't there. I don't—

BECKY: The girls were giving the boys blowjobs.

ROSE: Lucky them.

BECKY: Were you there, Rose?

ROSE: Were *you* there?

BECKY: Just tell me. I need to know.

ROSE: I said no.

BECKY: Did you know about this party?

ROSE: I'm not popular, Mom!

BECKY: Is that what it takes to be popular?

ROSE: Leave me alone.

BECKY: Have you ever given a boy a blowjob?

ROSE: What?

BECKY: Have you?

ROSE: You're sick.

BECKY: I need to know.

ROSE: How about this—you don't tell me when you give 'em, and I won't tell you when I give 'em.

BECKY: I just want you to know that you don't have to do anything you don't want to do.

ROSE: Good.

Rose starts to leave.

BECKY: I'm not done.

ROSE: I am.

BECKY: Where are you going?

ROSE: Outside. Jenny's dad'll be here any minute.

BECKY: You said you were going to Jenny's house.

ROSE: Are you deaf? I just said her dad's picking me up.

BECKY: But Jenny lives with her mom.

ROSE: What are you? A detective? She's at her dad's every other weekend.

BECKY: Where are you going tonight?

ROSE: Um, hello? Her dad's.

BECKY: No.

ROSE: What?

BECKY: No. No. No.

ROSE: What do you mean, no?

BECKY: I won't let you.

ROSE: Why not?

BECKY: You have to stay home.

ROSE: What?

BECKY: She can come here, but you can't go there.

ROSE: Have fun at work.

Rose starts to walk off. Becky gets in front of her, blocks the doorway.

BECKY: No. Stop.

ROSE: You can't make me stay here.

BECKY: Listen to me.

ROSE: As soon as you leave for work I'm out of here.

BECKY: Then I won't go to work.

ROSE: Fuck you.

BECKY: Rose.

68

ROSE: Sorry. I meant, "shit" you.

BECKY: I'm overprotective because I love you.

ROSE: You're so gay.

Becky tries to look Rose in the eyes. Rose looks away.

BECKY: And I don't want anything to happen to you.

ROSE: Can I go yet?

BECKY: I was too young when I gave my first blowjob.

ROSE: Shut up, that's sick, I don't want to hear that.

BECKY: I'm trying to tell you something so you can learn from my mistakes.

ROSE: How young were you?

BECKY: Younger than you.

ROSE: So you're a hypocrite?

BECKY: I was too young. I didn't understand what was happening.

And when he came in my mouth, it was such a shock.

ROSE: Oh my God.

BECKY: I cried. I cried and I threw up...

ROSE: I don't want to hear this.

BECKY: I just don't want you to do anything you're not ready for.

ROSE: Will you please stop talking?

BECKY: Promise me that? Will you? Promise me.

ROSE: I'm not listening to you.

BECKY: Promise me.

69

ROSE: No.

BECKY: If Carrie Turner has another party—

ROSE: I hate Carrie Turner.

BECKY: If she has another party—

ROSE: I hate her.

BECKY: —you're forbidden to go.

ROSE: I'm not popular, Mom. Carrie Turner hasn't spoken to me since the sixth grade. Girls like her don't look at me. They talk about me behind my back and they think I'm ugly and stupid and they definitely don't invite me to their parties. Which is fine with me. Because most of those guys are wretched. You couldn't pay me a million dollars to get near their dicks. They make me sick.

BECKY: Good.

The sound of a car horn honking outside.

ROSE: I'm going.

Becky stands aside. Rose runs off.

BLACKOUT.

SCENE THREE

Becky on stage, alone, in her dressing room at the strip club. Talking to the audience.

BECKY: Hi, my name's Becky.

How much time do I have? A minute?

Okay, I'll make this quick.

I've been listening to everything that you've all had to say and I think you all sound very smart.

That's all. That's all I want to share right now.

I'm sorry, my name's not Becky, it's Hunter. Hunter.

I chose it from a baby book because I played a game and that's the rule I made when I closed my eyes.

Sometimes you have to close your eyes and fall and just see where you land.

That's where my finger landed.

I made a rule. I got a book. And I played the game.

Simple.

Hunter: a two-syllable boy's name of Old English origin, means: One who searches or hunts. Entertainers with this name include Holly Hunter, Catfish Hunter, and Tab Hunter.

I don't even know who the fuck they are.

Fuck you.

No, fuck. You.

Fuck me.

Hello? Hello?

How *are* you? How are *you*?

What's your name?

What are you drinking?

You like that?

Huh?

Yeah, you like that?

You like my tits?

Are you comfortable?

Are you?

Are you?

Are you gonna be a piece of cake?

A piece of cock?

Is your cock hard?

Is it? Is it?

Can I feel it?

What about me, huh?

How much time do I have?

Thirty seconds?

Okay. Okay.

Make it good, Becky.

I mean, make it good, Hunter.

Just.

Make it. Just—

Are you going to leave me when this song ends?

Or do you want another?

Are you happy?

Am I making you happy?

Is that all you're gonna tip me?

What's your name? Huh? What's your—?

What's your poison?

What do you like?

What do you, what do you—?

Would you just tell me what you fucking like?

What you fucking, fucking, huh?

Time's up?

Fuck.

Fuck. Fuck.

Could you call me Hunter? Could you do that?

I've been waiting to tell someone my new name for quite some time.

BLACKOUT.

SCENE FOUR

At a STRIP CLUB.

*A small cubicle. Becky enters first,
followed by Elliot.*

BECKY: Have a seat.
ELLIOT: Okay.

He sits.

    Hi.
BECKY: Hi.
ELLIOT: Hi.
BECKY: Hello.
ELLIOT: Um. What's your name?
BECKY: Hunter.
ELLIOT: Really?
BECKY: Sure. What's yours?
ELLIOT: Tom.

BLACKOUT.

SCENE FIVE

Becky is in her cubicle. Brooke enters.

BECKY: Can I interest you in a lap dance?

BROOKE: Yes.

Music starts. Becky gives her a lapdance.
The music ends.

BROOKE: That was great.

BECKY: You've got beautiful eyes.

BROOKE: You move really well.

BECKY: You don't have to compliment me just because I
    complimented you.

BROOKE: I didn't.

BECKY: All you have to do is say thank you.

BROOKE: Thank you.

BECKY: What's your name?

BROOKE: Brooke.

BECKY: Brooke?

BROOKE: Actually, no. I don't know why I said that. That's my stage
    name.

BECKY: You're an actress?

BROOKE: No. I don't know why I said Brooke to you. I'm trying to
    be a stripper.

BECKY: Trying?

BROOKE: I mean, I am one. I just—. I just feel awkward.

BECKY: How so?

BROOKE: I feel like I'm not in my body. Like I don't know how to move correctly.

BECKY: How do you move?

BROOKE: It's just I'll be in the booth and I always feel like I'm bumping into the guy with my elbow.

BECKY: How bad is it?

BROOKE: I gave one guy a black eye.

BECKY: That's bad. How long?

BROOKE: I don't understand the question.

BECKY: How long have you been stripping?

BROOKE: I used to teach.

BECKY: Teach what?

BROOKE: I mean, not stripping. I didn't teach stripping.

BECKY: I didn't think you did.

BROOKE: I taught English. You know, to seventh graders.

BECKY: What happened?

BROOKE: It just got to be too much, you know? I got tired of kids. And it didn't pay well enough.

BECKY: So how long have you been stripping?

BROOKE: I really don't like kids when they're going through that whole adolescent thing. I'm sorry, I'm totally not answering your question. This is new. Stripping, stripping. It's definitely a new thing. I mean, I started with phone sex.

BECKY: Yeah?

BROOKE: Which led to the occasional trick?

BECKY: Did it?

BROOKE: Yeah.

BECKY: You seem so cavalier about that.

BROOKE: I don't know what I am about it, to be honest. I'm just telling you, that was what happened next.

BECKY: But when did you start stripping, you still haven't—

BROOKE: After that. One of my tricks introduced me to Moe.

BECKY: Who's Moe?

BROOKE: He manages the Pussycat.

BECKY: The Pussycat Theater?

BROOKE: No, The Pussycat Lounge.

BECKY: Never heard of it.

BROOKE: It's on 3rd.

BECKY: I don't know Moe.

BROOKE: Well, this trick of mine, he introduced me to Moe and that's when I started stripping.

BECKY: I don't hear the word "trick" that often.

BROOKE: I'm sorry, should I say "john"? I'm trying to get the lingo down.

BECKY: Say whatever you want.

BROOKE: I'm just trying not to be such a sore thumb all the time.

BECKY: Is the Pussycat full nude?

BROOKE: Yeah.

BECKY: I don't do full nude.

BROOKE: That's not what feels awkward. It's the—

BECKY: Movement?

BROOKE: Yeah. Still—

BECKY: Still what?

BROOKE: Sometimes I think it'd be nicer—

BECKY: To have the comfort of—

BROOKE: To know that the guys are drunk.

BECKY: I subbed for a girl at Southern Comfort once. That's full nude. I prefer pasties.

BROOKE: There's this one girl. She does a crab walk with her pussy. It's really amazing.

BECKY: Is her name Candace?

BROOKE: Yes!

BECKY: I know Candace.

BROOKE: Are you friends?

BECKY: No.

BROOKE: Because I think she has emotional problems.

BECKY: She's good though.

BROOKE: Yeah.

BECKY: She could teach you a thing or two.

BROOKE: I'm just kind of embarrassed to admit to the other girls at my club how awkward I feel. I thought it might be easier to get some help from a stranger.

BECKY: So you want some pointers.

BROOKE: I've been watching you.

BECKY: Yeah?

BROOKE: I think you're really good.

BECKY: Yeah.

BROOKE: And I want you to help me.

BECKY: Okay.

BROOKE: You'll do it?

BECKY: Sure.

BROOKE: How should we start?

BECKY: Well, first why don't you put your tits in my face and act like you mean it.

Loud music starts playing. Brooke begins to give Becky a lapdance. Rose enters.

ROSE: Mom?

BECKY: Rose?

BLACKOUT.

SCENE SIX

Rose is in her room, listening to very loud Nine Inch Nails (Track #2, "Wish" from their album Broken*). Either sprawled on the ground or on her bed— writing in her journal.*

Separately, Becky is in her room, sitting, her legs spread open, her head back, her arm in her mouth. Brooke is eating Becky out. Becky cums (stifling sounds). Brooke sits up in bed next to Becky.

BROOKE: You've got a lot of...

BECKY: What?

BROOKE: You know...

BECKY: Cum?

BROOKE: For a woman.

BECKY: I guess.

BROOKE: When was the last time you...

BECKY: Came?

BROOKE: Yeah.

BECKY: I don't know.

BROOKE: I've just never seen a woman...

BECKY: Cum so much?

BROOKE: Yeah.

BECKY: You're sweet.

BROOKE: Thanks.

BECKY: I mean that in the most unpatronizing way possible.

BROOKE: Okay.

BECKY: But I think it would be good for you to say it.

BROOKE: Say what?

BECKY: Any prostitute who's afraid to say the word "cum" has some issues she needs to deal with.

BROOKE: Cum.

BECKY: Was that so hard?

BROOKE: Your cum tastes really good.

BECKY: I just realized.

BROOKE: What?

BECKY: No. Never mind.

BROOKE: Tell me.

BECKY: The last time I came.

BROOKE: When was it?

BECKY: Is that music bothering you?

BROOKE: It's fine.

BECKY: No. No. No. Look, I'm sorry. This is inappropriate.

BROOKE: Why?

BECKY: This. This. I'm avoiding her.

BROOKE: The girl?

BECKY: She's my daughter.

BROOKE: I figured.

BECKY: I didn't want to face her.

BROOKE: After today?

BECKY: Would you?

BROOKE: She doesn't know what you do?

BECKY: She never asked.

Lights shift.

SCENE SEVEN

A moment later.

Rose's bedroom. Nine Inch Nails are blaring. (Same song. "Wish" from Broken.) Rose is furiously writing in her journal. Becky knocks on the door. Rose doesn't acknowledge it.

BECKY (*from off-stage*): Rose!

ROSE: Go away.

BECKY (*from off-stage*): Let me in Rose.

ROSE: What do you want?

BECKY (*from off-stage*): Let me in.

Rose gets off her bed, unlocks the door (but doesn't open it) and then gets back onto her bed. Becky opens the door, comes in. Rose has gone back to her writing.

BECKY (*yelling over the music*): What are you writing?

ROSE: Fuck you.

BECKY: Okay.

Becky switches off Rose's boom box.
Rose looks at her in disgust. Then goes
back to her writing. After a moment:

BECKY: I don't know what to say.

Rose ignores her.

BECKY: I'm sorry, Rose. You shouldn't have seen what you saw. I
should have told you what I did so you didn't have to be shocked
like that.

ROSE: I thought you were a dancer.

BECKY: I know.

ROSE: Do you know how I found out?

BECKY: No.

ROSE: Do you wanna know?

BECKY: Yes.

ROSE: You gave a lapdance to some guy who's in my Algebra class.
He saw you pick me up after school the other day and he
recognized you.

BECKY: I'm so sorry.

ROSE: He's a fucking retard.

BECKY: You shouldn't call people names.

ROSE: He won't stop staring at me in class.

BECKY: What did he say to you?

ROSE: He passed me a note.

BECKY: What did it say?

Rose pulls a wadded up piece of paper out of her pocket. She hands it to Becky. Becky un-wads it. She reads it.

BECKY: I'm sorry.

ROSE: Yeah. You are.

BECKY: This is mean.

ROSE: Is it true?

BECKY: Yes.

ROSE: I want you to tell me what you do.

BECKY: Really?

ROSE: Don't lie to me. Just tell me what you do.

BECKY: I'm a dancer. I take my clothes off. I give lap dances. I—

ROSE: What were you doing today?

BECKY: I was receiving a lapdance.

ROSE: I thought you gave them.

BECKY: Yes, usually that's what I do.

ROSE: But today you were getting one?

BECKY: Yes.

ROSE: Why?

BECKY: I'm sorry that I lied to you about what I did, but there are
    some things you don't need to know.

ROSE: Are you a lesbian?

BECKY: I don't think so, but if *you* are, that's okay.

85

ROSE: I'm not.

BECKY: I'll understand.

ROSE: I won't let you make this about me. It's about you.

BECKY: Okay.

ROSE: You're a freak.

BECKY: I'm trying, Rose. That's all I can do.

ROSE: Trying to be a ho?

BECKY: I'm trying to get us through. To guide you into adulthood without breaking you.

ROSE: I'm not an egg.

BECKY: Look, I'm sorry about what you saw tonight. I'm sorry I lied to you. What else can I say?

Beat.

BECKY: Is that a diary you're writing in?

ROSE: No.

BECKY: What is it?

ROSE: It's my journal.

BECKY: Rose, I'm sorry.

ROSE: I don't want to talk about it anymore.

BECKY: Okay.

ROSE: Leave me alone.

Beat. How long has it been since Becky's been in this room?

BECKY: Do you like any boys at school?

ROSE: What?

BECKY: I'm trying to have a conversation.

ROSE: Good luck.

BECKY: Maybe this boy in your Algebra class who wrote this note about me, maybe he wanted your attention because he likes you.

ROSE: That's the stupidest thing I've ever heard.

BECKY: So·you don't like him?

ROSE: No.

BECKY: Is there anyone else?

ROSE: There are guys that I like, yes, of course.

BECKY: Anyone specific?

ROSE: I have homework to do.

BECKY: Okay. Okay.

ROSE: So, like, leave.

BECKY: Okay, um. I need to know that we're cool before I go.

Rose doesn't respond.

BECKY: I want to make a deal with you.

ROSE: What kind of deal?

BECKY: No more lies. We share everything.

ROSE: You sure you want to know everything that goes on in my head?

BECKY: I think I can handle it.

ROSE: If I say yes, will you leave me alone?

BECKY: Yes.

ROSE: Yes.

BLACKOUT.

SCENE EIGHT

The strip club. Brooke has just finished giving Becky a lapdance.

BROOKE: Well?

BECKY: That was good.

BROOKE: Yeah?

BECKY: It was the best one so far.

BROOKE: You're not just saying that?

BECKY: No.

BROOKE: What can I do better?

BECKY: You can use your tits more.

BROOKE: Like how?

BECKY: Like you can touch them more. Push them around. Rub them into things.

BROOKE: Sometimes I feel so surreal.

BECKY: You don't like talking about your tits?

BROOKE: No.

She smiles, embarrassed.

You've taught me so much.

BECKY: No problem.

BROOKE: I wish I could reciprocate somehow.

BECKY: Please go away.

BROOKE: What?

BECKY: What what?

BROOKE: Why do you want me to go?

BECKY: I don't. Wait, what did you just—

BROOKE: Isn't that what you—

BECKY: No. What did you just say?

BROOKE: I said I wished I could reciprocate somehow.

BECKY: But you did. The other night.

BROOKE: But something more lasting. I feel like I'm in female training camp, like you're teaching me how to become a woman.

BECKY/FATHER'S VOICE: Your breasts are developing nicely.

BROOKE: What?

BECKY/FATHER'S VOICE: You're going to grow up to be a lovely woman one day.

BROOKE: What are you—

> *There is a knock on the door. Becky looks.*

BECKY (*violently*): It's occupied!

> *Brooke did not hear the knock. She looks at Becky oddly.*

BROOKE: Are you okay?

BECKY: Yes.

BROOKE: I guess I'm just trying to say thank you. Thank you for everything.

BECKY: You're welcome.

BROOKE: Because I've been feeling less awkward. And I guess it does feel like I'm becoming a woman.

There is another knock on the door.

FATHER'S VOICE: Becky.

BECKY: What do you want?

FATHER'S VOICE: Your mother has a headache.

BECKY: I'm not here.

FATHER'S VOICE: Can I come in?

BECKY: Get the fuck out of here! I'm busy!

BROOKE: What? Why? What are you—?

BECKY: No, not you. *Him.*

BROOKE: Who?

BECKY: It's okay.

FATHER'S VOICE: You have to let me do what I want to you because I made you and you belong to me.

BECKY (*yelling towards the voice*): You touch me again and I'll kill you!

(*To Brooke*)

If we just stay quiet, he might leave.

BROOKE: Who?

BECKY: If he comes in here, play dead.

BROOKE: Are you okay?

BECKY: Be quiet.

BROOKE: But there's no one.

BECKY: You don't hear that?

BROOKE: Hear what?

BECKY: That man.

BROOKE: There's no man.

BECKY: Are you sure?

> *Brooke goes to the door, looks.*

BROOKE: There's no man.

BECKY: You're sure?

BROOKE: Yes.

> *Becky goes to the door and double-checks. She starts crying.*

BROOKE: What's wrong?

BECKY (*under her breathe*): I hope that motherfucker is dead.

BROOKE: Who?

BECKY (*changing subject, urgent*): If Brooke's your stage name, what's your real name?

BROOKE: Kristen.

BECKY: Hi Kristen, I'm really Becky, not Hunter.

KRISTEN: I know. You told me.

BECKY: Did I?

KRISTEN: It's okay.

BECKY: I'm sorry to be like this. I'm okay, I'm okay.

KRISTEN: Let me get you something to eat.

BECKY: It's like deja-vu, but it feels more real—like my skin
    remembers, not just my head. But I'm okay.

KRISTEN: You're okay.

BECKY: I am.

KRISTEN: When do you get off?

BECKY: Two.

KRISTEN: Let me take you out then. Late dinner, early breakfast.
    Your choice. I'll come back and pick you up.

BECKY: Really?

KRISTEN: My treat.

BECKY: No, I couldn't.

KRISTEN: But you will. Please. I want to.

BECKY: Okay.

KRISTEN: Okay?

BECKY: Okay.

BLACKOUT.

SCENE NINE

Same cubicle, a few minutes later. Becky is alone. Rose enters.

ROSE: Mom?

BECKY: Rose? What are you doing here?

ROSE: I need to talk to you.

BECKY: Really?

ROSE: This place smells like sweat.

BECKY: What's wrong?

ROSE: Your cell phone isn't on.

BECKY: You're supposed to call and have them page me.

ROSE: He wouldn't.

BECKY: Who wouldn't? Steve?

ROSE: No, the other guy.

BECKY: Sam?

ROSE: I don't know.

BECKY: That was Sam. Next time you call him, you tell him it's an emergency. What's wrong?

ROSE: Do we have to talk here?

BECKY: Where do you want to go?

ROSE: Someplace private.

BECKY: We're in a private booth. This is as much privacy as we're gonna get here.

ROSE: I don't want to be here.

BECKY: Just tell me what's wrong.

ROSE: I don't know.

BECKY: Talk to me Rose.

ROSE: I think I'm sick.

BECKY: Sick how? What hurts?

ROSE: I threw up.

BECKY: Do you have a fever?

ROSE: No.

BECKY: Let me feel you.

> *She puts the back of her hand on Rose's forehead.*

You don't feel hot.

ROSE: I'm fine, never mind.

> *She begins to go.*

BECKY: Rose, no. What's wrong?

ROSE: I don't know.

BECKY: Why do you feel sick?

ROSE: I told you I don't know!

BECKY: Rose, tell me what hurts.

ROSE: My stomach.

BECKY: Okay, good, what else?

ROSE: I don't know.

BECKY: When did you throw up?

ROSE: Yesterday. Today. The day before yesterday. I don't know.

BECKY: You don't remember?

ROSE: I told you. All of those days, okay?

BECKY: Are you making yourself do it?

ROSE: I'm not a fucking anorexic.

BECKY: How long have you been throwing up?

ROSE: A while.

BECKY: Why haven't you told me you were sick before?

ROSE: I just did.

BECKY: Okay, then. Rose?

ROSE: What?

BECKY: When was your last period?

No response. Beat.

Rose? When was your last period?

ROSE: I don't know.

BECKY: You don't *know* or you don't remember?

ROSE: Two months ago.

BECKY (*breathing in deep*): Okay. Okay. Do you have a boyfriend?

ROSE: No.

BECKY: Okay. Do you—*did you* have a boyfriend?

ROSE: When?

BECKY: Two months ago.

ROSE: Yes.

BECKY: Okay. And he didn't—he didn't make you do anything you
    didn't want to do, did he?

ROSE: No, he didn't—

BECKY: I mean, he didn't force you, did he?

ROSE: No.

BECKY: Did he?

ROSE: No. I promise you. *I* forced *him*.

BECKY: Okay. Okay.

ROSE: Are you gonna kill me?

BECKY: Are you sure about your period?

ROSE: Yes.

BECKY: Okay. Have you taken a test?

ROSE: No.

BECKY: Okay. Then let's go to Rite Aid.

ROSE: You're not gonna kill me?

BECKY: Let's go to Rite Aid.

BLACKOUT.

SCENE TEN

A deep base beat pumps through the sound system. Elliot is sitting in a large overstuffed red loveseat. Becky stands over him, swaying her hips to the beat of the bump.

She rides his knee. Thumping and pumping and blow-your-house-down-ing.

She unbuttons her blouse, takes it off, revealing two butterfly pasties. She rubs her hands through Elliot's hair, pushes his head into her bosom.

ELLIOT: Stop.

BECKY: What?

ELLIOT: This is too weird.

BECKY: Am I being too rough? You don't want me to touch your head? What?

ELLIOT: Becky, it's me.

BECKY: It fucking is.

ELLIOT: I wasn't sure if you recognized me.

BECKY: I didn't the first time.

ELLIOT: I didn't recognize you.

BECKY: I didn't know until you said my name.

ELLIOT: Becky. Hi Becky.

BECKY: Hi Elliot.

ELLIOT: So.

BECKY: Yeah.

ELLIOT: Wow.

BECKY: Should I put my top back on?

ELLIOT: I don't know.

BECKY: My job doesn't usually make me feel dirty.

ELLIOT: I'm sorry.

BECKY: But right now...

ELLIOT: I don't know what to say.

BECKY: I know.

ELLIOT: Will you put your shirt back on? I don't want to look at your
    boobs.

> *Becky puts her top on. She takes a long*
> *look at Elliot.*

BECKY: You look different.

ELLIOT: You too.

BECKY: You didn't used to have facial hair.

ELLIOT: No.

BECKY (*a sudden realization*): You shave.

ELLIOT: Not lately.

BECKY: But you can.

ELLIOT: Yeah.

BECKY: That blows my mind.

ELLIOT: It's been awhile.

BECKY: You should shave.

ELLIOT: I don't really feel like it.

BECKY: Since you can.

ELLIOT: I'm lazy.

BECKY: You'd look better.

ELLIOT: You can't be gone for fifteen years and then just tell me what to do all of a sudden.

BECKY: It hasn't been that long.

ELLIOT: Yes it has.

BECKY: No it hasn't.

ELLIOT: You wanna bet?

BECKY: Not really.

ELLIOT: It's been fifteen years.

BECKY: Are you sure?

ELLIOT: Yes.

BECKY: I don't believe you.

ELLIOT: It's true.

BECKY: It can't be.

ELLIOT: It can and it is.

BECKY: Shit.

ELLIOT: I know.

BECKY: How can you look so different and so the same and how can it be fifteen years, I don't believe it.

ELLIOT: Your hair's different.

BECKY: What was it before?

ELLIOT: Longer.

BECKY: I cut it.

ELLIOT: Right.

BECKY: Yeah.

ELLIOT: There's something else.

BECKY: What?

ELLIOT: Am I crazy or didn't your eyes used to be blue?

BECKY: They did.

ELLIOT: But now they're brown.

BECKY: Contacts.

ELLIOT: Of course.

BECKY: You?

ELLIOT: What?

BECKY: You had glasses before.

ELLIOT: Yeah.

BECKY: So now you've got lenses too.

ELLIOT: No, I just started feeling self-conscious about the glasses so I stopped wearing them and now I don't see very well.

BECKY: Oh.

ELLIOT: After fifteen years, there's got to be something more important to talk about.

BECKY: We're rusty, that's all.

ELLIOT: Right.

Neither of them says anything for a long moment.

ELLIOT: Well...

BECKY: Well what?

ELLIOT: Don't you have anything to say?

BECKY: Like what?

ELLIOT: Like why didn't you ever call?

BECKY: Why?

ELLIOT: To let me know you were okay.

BECKY: There were things.

ELLIOT: Yeah?

BECKY: Things I should tell you now, I guess, but things I couldn't say then.

ELLIOT: Shoot.

BECKY: First, I'm dying—

ELLIOT: You're dying?

BECKY: No. I'm dying to know—

ELLIOT: Oh. What?

BECKY: How's mom?

BLACKOUT.

End of Act Two. Intermission.

ACT THREE

SCENE ONE

LIGHTS UP. Mom is alone onstage. Waiting in Elliot's living room. She has her eyes closed. She's humming to herself, going over a Bjork tune.

Elliot enters.

ELLIOT: She's up, she's just—. She'll be out in a minute.

MOM: I need to talk to you.

ELLIOT: I'm gonna be late for work.

MOM: I need to talk to you about your father.

ELLIOT: I don't want to talk about him.

MOM: Okay. There's just something I need to tell you.

ELLIOT: Not when B's about to come in.

MOM: Maybe when you get home?

ELLIOT: Maybe.

MOM: After work?

ELLIOT: *Mom.*

Beat.

ELLIOT: We're out of cereal.

MOM: That's fine, I'll—

ELLIOT: We have eggs.

MOM: I know.

Little B enters.

MOM: There's my little girl.

ELLIOT: Okay, be good, B. I'll see you guys later.

MOM: Just—

> *Mom stops him. Fixes his collar, or wipes something off his cheek, or some other act of motherly care.*
>
> *Elliot leaves. Mom takes a CD case [Bjork's "Debut"] out of her purse.*

MOM: This is for you. You know what this is?

> *Little B nods.*

MOM: I've been practicing. I couldn't understand all of the lyrics, so I used the internet. You ready?

Little B nods. Mom sings "Come To Me"
[track #? on "Debut"] by Bjork.

MOM (*a capella*): "You know / That I adore you / You know / That I love you / So don't make me say it / It would burst the bubble / Break the charm / Jump off / Your building's on fire / I'll catch you / I'll catch you / Destroy all that is keeping you back / And then I'll nurse you / I'll nurse you / Come to me / I'll take care of you / You don't have to explain / I understand."

Little B hugs her, thank you.

MOM (*to Little B*): Sometimes a child stays a child, by sheer force of will.
LITTLE B (*to Mom*): "Okay, then,"

Then Little B begins a ritual. It's something she does to calm the storm in her head, when the noises and other stimuli of the world get to be too much. She stands on an imagined precipice. Once there, she begins throwing off car parts and bottles and cutlery. For those who know B, this is not an uncommon sight, this is not unusual.

MOM: And sometimes a child stays a child by...other forces.

LITTLE B: "Now that we're alone, we can talk."

MOM: Sometimes a thing will happen right under our noses—this thing might happen to our children—this thing that happened to us when we were children—or to some of us—

LITTLE B: "Okay, then,"

MOM: —in particular...to think that something like this could happen without, without seeing any of the clues—and that's not for a lack of trying—we're all trying—and it's not for a lack of will, or willpower—

LITTLE B: "I think I'll be singing until I die,"

MOM: It's just that sometimes the past slips into the present—

LITTLE B: "About ninety years old."

MOM: —without our realizing it.

LITTLE B: "...if I have any vision of life."

MOM: And that can be the most unfathomable thing in the world.

LITTLE B: "Sometimes it's quite weird because I try to get away from it, but no matter how far I try to go, I always somehow get back to it."

MOM: Uh, huh. Yeah...I have this hope, this dream, this wish, this fear, this desire—

LITTLE B: "It's an obsession."

MOM: This, yes. Yes. It's this idea that maybe time doesn't move forward like we think it does—now I've thought about this a lot and I don't even quite understand it myself, so I'm not sure that I'll be able to explain it to you. But what if today doesn't follow yesterday and tomorrow today? What if tomorrow happened two years ago and today is really going to happen several weeks from now? The part of this idea that excites me is the possibility that maybe we could live all of the bad days of our lives consecutively—and then when they're done, they'll really be done—and the rest; well the rest...that's what we'd look forward to...But this is all hypothetical—

LITTLE B: "I'm still learning, but I've got 55 years to live, so I'm hoping to get it sorted out by around the year 2050...When you're obsessed with something, you can explain it five years later, but in the moment, you don't know exactly why...The thing is, I just HAVE to write songs, almost to even the pressure out. It's like if I create a song, then I have a replica outside me of what I'm hearing inside, and it sort of evens out the pressure. That is quite a physical, almost selfish, thing and it's as important to me as it is to eat or sleep."

MOM: —Reality is...more difficult, I suppose.

FATHER'S VOICE: Little B?

LITTLE B (*ignoring him*): "When I walk outside and I'm singing and I can hear all the music in my head—

FATHER'S VOICE: Little B?

LITTLE B (*ignoring him*): "It's just a very generous, joyous place to be, and there's nothing wrong with it."

FATHER'S VOICE: Little B?

LITTLE B (*ignoring him*): "As a kid I was an extreme introvert; I sometimes wouldn't speak to people for days, but I'd be euphoric.

MOM: I remember.

FATHER'S VOICE: Little B?

LITTLE B (*ignoring him*): "I was lucky because nobody told me there was anything wrong with me. Actually, I think that most people are pretty introverted—they just hide it really well."

FATHER'S VOICE: Little B?

> *Beat.*

> *For the first time, Mom and Little B both look in the direction of the voice. They try to remain as still as possible, waiting for the voice to give up and retreat.*

FATHER'S VOICE: Little B?
  Little B?
  Little B?
  Little B?

> *Silence.*

> *Little B and Mom hold hands. Little B looks out over the edge of the precipice.*

Mom looks at her daughter.

MOM: Now let's get to matters of the heart.

BLACKOUT.

SCENE TWO

Little B, alone on stage, to the audience.

She begins as "Bjork," but by the time she says "He's sitting across from me at the dinner table," she has lost that mask.

She is like a child who has scraped her knee and doesn't know to cry because she hasn't yet seen an adult's worried response.

[If we think of this monologue as having a time and a place, it is: Three years ago. Little B is twelve. She is talking to her mother. They are in the living room. The worst, the final, act of abuse by her father has taken place. But we're not exactly living in the physical world here. It should simultaneously feel like a memory and like something that Little B is living as she speaks it. It's a purging, a vomit of emotion.]

[Sound Cue: At some point, towards the end of the monologue, Little B might hear snippets of the Mike/Elliot scene coming from offstage.]

LITTLE B: Hi.

Hello.

Hi.

Hi.

Now that we're alone we can talk.

My name is—

I'm sorry, could you just—

Um.

Could you excuse me for a moment?

Just between you and me.

Now that we're alone.

Just between you and...

Beat.

He's sitting across from me at the dinner table.

I'm twelve years old.

Becky's been gone since before I was born.

And Elliot's been gone for a couple years now.

It's just Mom and him and me—

just him and Mom and me

just him and me

just him and me

111

just him

and

him

and

him. And me.

I'm sitting here—

Mom's in the kitchen, she's cooking

and she's singing, I can hear her singing:

"Momma's in the kitchen with shortnen, shortnen, Momma's in

the kitchen with shortnen bread."

He's looking at me. He says,

"One day. One day it'll happen."

Hi.

Hello.

Hi.

I just want him to love me.

I'm looking into his eyes. I want to open my mouth to say

something.

But I can't.

We're staring at each other—

Beat.

And he says it again.

"One day. One day it'll happen."

I feel so...

I'm so—

And he's so—

So...so...

This secret that we share, it feels like,

like our destiny.

And his words—. And his words—.

How they sound on his lips.

He says them like they're stone.

(*the following in one breath*)

I

am

holding

my breath

so as not to

make a sound,

so that I won't

miss anything else

he might say that might

help me understand what

he means.

(*exhale*)

Mom's singing in the kitchen again:

"Momma's little angel likes shortnen, shortnen. Momma's little angel likes shortnen bread."

I'm not looking at his eyes any more. I can't.

I don't want to look up, but I don't know how not to.

BLACKOUT.

SCENE THREE

This scene takes place after the Mike/Elliot scene. We're in Elliot's bedroom. Elliot's awake. Little B enters.

LITTLE B: Elliot?

ELLIOT: What's wrong, B?

LITTLE B: I can't sleep.

ELLIOT: Why not?

LITTLE B: Was dad in here?

ELLIOT: When?

LITTLE B: I thought I just heard him.

ELLIOT: Did you see him?

LITTLE B: No.

ELLIOT: It wasn't dad.

LITTLE B: Then who was it?

ELLIOT: No more questions B.

FATHER'S VOICE: Little B.

LITTLE B *(ignoring him)*: "I used to work in a fish factory, listening to music and making rhythms."

ELLIOT: Little B.

FATHER'S VOICE: Little B.

LITTLE B *(ignoring him):* "Growing up, I saw The Sound of Music twenty times because it was the only film we had in our little town."

ELLIOT: Why do you have to do this?

LITTLE B: "Because I am very stubborn when I get an idea."

ELLIOT: B, would you snap out of it? Little B?

FATHER'S VOICE: Little B, it's your father.

LITTLE B: Lights!

> *The lights change and we are inside Little B's head.*

FATHER'S VOICE: Can I come in?

> *From Little B's body language we can tell that Father has entered the room. (But we do not see him.)*

LITTLE B (*singing*): Raindrops on roses and whiskers on kittens,

FATHER'S VOICE: Little B?

> *He's approaching her.*

LITTLE B: Bright copper kettles and warm woolen mittens,

FATHER'S VOICE: Look at me, Little B.

> *He's touching her, fondling her. For a moment, she's not sure if she can go on...*

LITTLE B: Brother!

Elliot enters the fantasy.

LITTLE B and ELLIOT: Brown paper packages tied up with string,
FATHER'S VOICE: Little B?
LITTLE B and ELLIOT: These are a few of my favorite things.
FATHER'S VOICE: Why don't you look at me, Little B.
LITTLE B and ELLIOT: Cream colored ponies and crisp apple strudel,
    doorbells and sleigh bells and schnitzel with noodles,
LITTLE B: Mother!

Mom enters the fantasy.

LITTLE B/ELLIOT/MOM: Wild geese that fly with the moon on their
    wings, these are a few of my favorite things.
FATHER'S VOICE: I'm going to count to three.

Little B is unable to continue singing.
She summons her sister for more help.

LITTLE B: Sister!

Becky enters (or Little B's fantasy of who
Becky is, since they've never met and her
only experience with Becky is through a

fifteen-year-old photo.)

*Mom, Elliot, and Becky try to keep the
song going, to get B out of her head and
back into the song.*

MOM/BECKY/ELLIOT: Girls in white dresses with blue satin sashes.

FATHER'S VOICE: And then you're going to look at me.

MOM/BECKY/ELLIOT: Snowflakes that stay on your nose and
    eyelashes.

FATHER'S VOICE: One.

MOM/BECKY/ELLIOT: Silver white winters that melt into spring.

FATHER'S VOICE: Two.

MOM/BECKY/ELLIOT: These are a few of your favorite things.

FATHER'S VOICE: Three.

Little B struggles back, rejoining Mom.

LITTLE B/MOM/BECKY/ELLIOT: When the dog barks.

FATHER'S VOICE: Little B.

LITTLE B/MOM/BECKY/ELLIOT: When the bee stings.

FATHER'S VOICE: Little B.

LITTLE B/MOM/BECKY/ELLIOT: When I'm feeling sad.

FATHER'S VOICE: Little B.

LITTLE B/MOM/BECKY/ELLIOT: I simply remember my favorite
    things, and then I don't feel so bad.

FATHER'S VOICE: Don't you have anything to say to your father?
MOM: Is he gone yet?
LITTLE B: No.

Little B leads them all in another round of the song. They sing it forcefully, as if it were an exorcism. [Double time.] Physically, Little B is still trying to fight off her father.

LITTLE B/MOM/BECKY/ELLIOT:	FATHER'S VOICE:
Raindrops on roses and whiskers on kittens. Bright copper kettles and warm woolen mittens. Brown paper packages tied up with string. These are a few of my favorite things. Cream colored ponies and crisp apple strudel, doorbells and sleigh bells and schnitzel with noodles, wild geese that fly with the moon on their wings, these are a few of my favorite things. When the dog bites, when the bee stings, when I'm feeling sad. I simply remember my favorite things, and then I don't feel so— BAD!	(*continuing throughout the song...*) Little B. Little B. Little B. (*they are all trying to drown out his voice*) Elliot. Becky. Little B. Let me in. Elliot. Becky. Little B. Let me in. Little—

Little B pushes her father off her, out of the room. She lets out a primal scream.

The lights return to normal. Everyone else is gone, except for Elliot, who tries to comfort Little B.

ELLIOT: Little B?

LITTLE B: Don't touch me.

ELLIOT: Okay. You're all right, you know. He's gone.

LITTLE B: Where?

ELLIOT: Dying.

LITTLE B: "I know everybody thinks I'm completely mad and a lunatic, but in Iceland, believe me, I'm the quiet one."

ELLIOT: Okay.

LITTLE B: You're supposed to protect me.

ELLIOT: I'm trying.

LITTLE B: He was here.

She points to her head.

And here.

She points to her heart.

ELLIOT: He'll go.

LITTLE B: Did he go for you?

ELLIOT: You should get some sleep, B.

LITTLE B: Who was the man?

ELLIOT: A friend. A boy.

LITTLE B: I don't like him.

ELLIOT: Just forget about him then. He won't be back.

> *Little B begins to fade into sleepiness.*
> *Elliot tries to usher her back to her*
> *room.*

LITTLE B: "When I was fourteen, I thought boys were only good for
   being in bands with."

ELLIOT: What do you think now?

LITTLE B: Can I sleep in here?

ELLIOT: Okay.

LITTLE B: "After this, I'm living by the ocean. My mother, the
   ocean."

ELLIOT: You're tired and from now on you're not eating any sugar in
   the middle of the night.

LITTLE B: "I think my music has always been for headphones and
   people to listen to in private."

ELLIOT: Okay. Go to sleep.

LITTLE B: "I'm only here for a period."

ELLIOT: I know. Now sleep.

LITTLE B: "To get my mission done."

ELLIOT: That's right. Sleep.

LITTLE B (*she is falling asleep*): "And once it's finished, it's finished."

ELLIOT: Okay.

He takes her—almost asleep—to bed.

BLACKOUT.

SCENE FOUR

Elliot's house. Elliot, Little B, and Becky.

BECKY: Why won't she say anything to me?

ELLIOT: She's heard so much about you...you're like, I don't know, Santa Claus. Someone you don't expect to ever actually come face to face with.

BECKY: I'm her sister.

ELLIOT: Let her get used to you.

BECKY: If he wasn't already dying, I'd kill him for doing this to her.

ELLIOT: Yeah, well.

Beat.

BECKY: I have a daughter her age, you know.

ELLIOT: You do?

BECKY: Yeah.

ELLIOT: Fifteen?

BECKY: Yeah.

ELLIOT: Jesus. I—

BECKY: Don't.

ELLIOT: What's her name?

BECKY: Rose.

Beat.

ELLIOT: Look, do you want a beer or something?

BECKY: Please.

ELLIOT: I'll be right back.

Elliot goes out. Little B looks at Becky.

LITTLE B: Can I touch you?

BECKY: Where?

LITTLE B: Your hand.

BECKY: Sure.

Little B takes Becky's hand. Feels it,
looks at it.

LITTLE B: My mother, the ocean, loves me more than anything. She
hates to be separated from me, but that's the way things have to
be.

BECKY: She's my mother too.

LITTLE B: I know.

BECKY: I know he hurt you bad.

Little B looks away. Beat.

BECKY: Look, I'm...I'm sorry I ran away. But then again, it seems to
me like they never would've had you if I hadn't. So that's gotta
be a good thing, right? I know right now you probably don't see

the good in that, you probably wish you'd never been born, but believe me, even with all of the bad, I can tell that you're a good thing. And I'm sorry I missed fifteen years of you.

Beat.

Look, are you gonna say anything?

Beat.

You and my daughter might get along. She doesn't speak to me either. She's, what—your niece, I guess? Or she's your—. Oh, that's fucked up. I can't even finish the thought it's so fucked up. Shit, I didn't mean to swear. Don't listen to me. And if you, you know, ever end up actually speaking, and Rose happens to be in the room, don't tell her I said 'fuck.' Or no, you know what? Do tell her, I don't know. Maybe if she heard me say 'fuck' once in awhile, she'd give me some respect...

> *At some point during the following, Elliot comes to the door. Becky doesn't see him. Elliot stays back and listens.*

I'm afraid I've completely failed as a parent...Do you know what it feels like to be so bad at something? She's pregnant and I just...I know it's different. I know she and I are different. Her life is much better and she doesn't know that, and she, she, she hates me, you know, and she's difficult, but she really is a good kid...You're my sister. Jesus Christ, you're my motherfucking sister. That's just so unreal. I can't tell you how many times— when we were kids—I wished I had a sister instead of a brother, and now I have you. But Elliot was good to have back then. He was. But you know, all of those years I was protecting him...it was happening and I didn't say anything because I thought it would keep him safe...all of those years, I had no idea. I had no idea. And now I look back on it and I think, how stupid. Like maybe if we didn't spend so much time trying not to hurt each other, then maybe we wouldn't hurt each other so much. Because I think Elliot was doing the same thing. He was trying to keep me safe. And I love him and I hate him for that...Do you have anything to say yet? It's fine if you don't. I'm a good talker. Listen, if you're never able to talk to me, I'm still glad our brother found me and now I know you exist and we can sit next to each other and just be sisters...Hey, do you know if our brother is gay? It's fine if he is because I think I might be too. Funny, huh? I'm not really sure. But it's the vibe I get from him and I know we only just found each other again, but if it is true, I wish he'd tell me so. I just don't want to waste any more time with him. We have to stop running away from the truth. That's all. I love you. Little B, I love you. Oh man, you know, if you don't start holding up your end of the conversation, I could talk forever...Eh?

LITTLE B: I think he is too.

BECKY: Really.

LITTLE B: Yes.

Elliot clears his throat, enters.

ELLIOT: Beer.

(*To Little B*)

Soda.

BECKY: Took you long enough.

ELLIOT: It was in the back of the fridge.

He hands Becky a beer and Little B an orange cola. He also has a beer for himself. They all simultaneously take a swig.

BECKY: Elliot, do you think she'll want to see me?

ELLIOT: Yes.

BECKY: You don't think she hates me, do you?

ELLIOT: No.

BECKY: For leaving.

ELLIOT: Mom loves you.

BECKY: Do you hate me?

ELLIOT: No.

BECKY: I've decided it's best to get all of my worries out in the air instead of keeping them inside.

LITTLE B: She talks about you a lot.

They each take a swig of their drinks.

BECKY: Hey, B, what's the B stand for?

LITTLE B: Bjork.

Beat.

ELLIOT: Becky.

LITTLE B and BECKY: What?

ELLIOT: The B stands for Becky.

BLACKOUT.

End of Act Three.

ACT FOUR

SCENE ONE

Rose and Becky's kitchen. Rose and Elliot sit together, awkward. Elliot is staring at her.

ROSE: Stop looking at me like that.

ELLIOT: This is crazy.

ROSE: Do you have to keep saying that?

ELLIOT: I just can't get over it.

ROSE: Okay.

ELLIOT: I can't believe it.

ROSE: You said that already.

ELLIOT: Sorry.

ROSE: She never told me about you either.

ELLIOT: Really?

ROSE: I never knew I had an uncle.

ELLIOT: That's fucked up.

ROSE: A lot of things are fucked up.

ELLIOT: Yeah, I guess they are.

ROSE: So she just left?

ELLIOT: When?

ROSE: Whenever she left.

ELLIOT: Yeah, she just...

ROSE: Left.

ELLIOT: Yeah.

ROSE: Doesn't that make you mad?

ELLIOT: I don't know.

ROSE: Don't you wanna kill her?

ELLIOT: Not really.

ROSE: I wish she was dead sometimes.

ELLIOT: Really?

ROSE: Yeah. I don't know that I'd wanna kill her, but sometimes I wish she was dead.

ELLIOT: But she's your mom.

ROSE: I don't care.

ELLIOT: My mom does crazy things but I never wish she was dead.

ROSE: You're joking, right?

ELLIOT: No.

ROSE: But there are other people you wish were dead, aren't there?

ELLIOT (*after a moment*): Yeah. There's one.

ROSE: I told you.

ELLIOT: But your mom's a good person.

ROSE: Do you know what she does?

ELLIOT: Yeah.

ROSE: For a living?

ELLIOT: I know.

ROSE: She's a stripper.

ELLIOT: Yeah.

ROSE: She's stripping right now.

ELLIOT: There are worse things.

ROSE: I don't know.

ELLIOT: Believe me.

ROSE: What are you doing here exactly?

ELLIOT: What do you mean?

ROSE: I mean, is she making you stay here with me to keep an eye on me?

ELLIOT: Like am I babysitting you?

ROSE: Yeah.

ELLIOT: I don't do things like that. Baby-sit. I'm too old.

ROSE: Then why are you here?

ELLIOT: I don't know.

ROSE: You don't know?

ELLIOT: I guess I just thought I'd try to be an uncle.

ROSE: Really?

ELLIOT: Yeah.

ROSE: An uncle.

ELLIOT: Since I am one.

ROSE: You really expect me to believe that?

ELLIOT: I do that too.

ROSE: Do what?

ELLIOT: Say "really" a lot

ROSE: Really?

ELLIOT: Yeah. I say it a lot.

ROSE: Really?

ELLIOT: Yeah.

ROSE: So you're just here because you want to be my uncle?

ELLIOT: Yeah.

ROSE: Okay.

ELLIOT: Hey, do you know what uncles do, by any chance?

ROSE: No.

ELLIOT: Just checking.

ROSE: Wait a second.

ELLIOT: What?

ROSE: I just heard you.

ELLIOT: What?

ROSE: You said that your mom does crazy things.

ELLIOT: So?

ROSE: That means I have a grandmother too?

ELLIOT: Yeah.

ROSE: This is so fucked up.

ELLIOT: Why?

ROSE: She doesn't tell me anything. Do I have a grandfather?

ELLIOT: Sort of.

ROSE: What's that mean?

ELLIOT: He's dying.

ROSE: Really?

ELLIOT: Cancer.

ROSE: How bad is it?

ELLIOT: Pretty bad.

ROSE: Fuck.

She opens up her journal and begins to write furiously, ignoring Elliot. He watches her.

ROSE: Do you mind?

ELLIOT: Sorry.

He looks away from her. After a moment.

ELLIOT: Hey.

ROSE: What?

ELLIOT: You wanna play a game?

ROSE: What kind of game?

ELLIOT: It's a game your mom and I played when we were kids.

ROSE: Okay I guess.

ELLIOT: That's your journal, right?

ROSE: Why?

ELLIOT: Just trust me, I'm not gonna—it *is* your journal, right?

ROSE: Yeah.

ELLIOT: Okay, would you be willing to share one sentence in that journal with me?

ROSE: Why?

ELLIOT: It's something Becky and I used to do. I mean, your mom. Becky—your mom. That sounds so strange. Anyway, we both had journals, right? And we'd play this game. I'd randomly choose a sentence from Becky's journal and she'd randomly choose one from mine. Then we'd read the sentences out loud.

ROSE: I don't know.

ELLIOT: It'll be fun.

ROSE: But that's not fair.

ELLIOT: Why not?

ROSE: You don't have a journal. It would just be me.

ELLIOT: Next time I come over, I promise to bring my journal.

ROSE: I don't know.

ELLIOT: How about we play the game and then you read the sentence
     to yourself first? And if it's something you don't want to read,
     you don't have to.

ROSE: Okay.

ELLIOT: So start flipping through the pages in your journal and I'll
     tell you when to stop.

She does.

ELLIOT: Stop. Okay, now go back and forth between those two pages
     and I'll tell you when to stop.

She does.

ELLIOT: Okay, stop. Now go up and down that page with your finger
     and I'll say stop.

She does.

ELLIOT: Stop. Okay, now read that sentence to yourself.

She does.

ROSE: Okay, I read it.

ELLIOT: And?

ROSE: I don't want to read it to you.

ELLIOT: That's what Becky always said.

ROSE: Really?

ELLIOT: Really.

BLACKOUT.

SCENE TWO

Little B's room. Rose and Little B sit together, awkwardly.

ROSE: So I can't believe you're, like, my aunt.

No response.

ROSE: Can you talk?

LITTLE B: Yes.

ROSE: How old are you?

LITTLE B: I don't know.

ROSE: Okay.

Beat. Rose stares at Little B. Little B avoids eye contact.

ROSE: My mom said your name was Little B. What's the "B" stand for?

LITTLE B: Bjork.

ROSE: Like the singer?

LITTLE B: I *am* the singer.

ROSE: You're *the* Bjork?

LITTLE B: Yes.

ROSE: Are you crazy?

LITTLE B: No.

ROSE: Then what are you?

LITTLE B: I'm Bjork.

ROSE: Okay.

> *Rose stares at Little B, like, 'Are you joking?'*

ROSE: So, *Bjork—*

LITTLE B: Yes?

ROSE: What kind of music do you like?

LITTLE B: What do you mean?

ROSE: Like what do you listen to?

LITTLE B: Music.

ROSE: But what do you listen to?

> *No response.*

ROSE: Can I see your Walkman?

> *Little B hands it to her. Rose opens it, takes the CD out and looks at it.*

ROSE: This is Bjork.

LITTLE B: Yes.

ROSE: You're listening to yourself?

LITTLE B: That's my music.

ROSE: Okay. But what music do you listen to? I mean, other than this.

LITTLE B: "I get shy attacks. Part of it is that I come from a very working-class family and from a communal household in Iceland where there never was such a thing as hierarchy. Artists are on the same level as plumbers. They're all the same. And then, when I was 14, punk happened, and I got very involved with anarchy and the idea that nobody tells another person what to do—everybody's equal and you can encourage people to be as much as they are. Even though it's a capital in Europe, Reykjavik, where I grew up, is like a small village. It's full of eccentrics, and it has that small-town thing where you know everyone. You go to the supermarket and you meet a painter and a fisherman, and then you meet the president and a taxi driver. Another way to answer the question is that my hero as a child was David Attenborough because he introduced nature to the living room, you know? He lifted up a rock and it was full of worlds you'd never seen, like ants, and he'd tell you they're all having sex or something. It looked really boring, but when he told you the story, it was amazing. So I guess I've always been fascinated by the kind of person who introduces one world to another. I think if you ask a person on the street what they listen to, most would say, 'Oh, I like everything.' They hear jazz in a taxi, and then they go home and listen to heavy metal. I think all of us want to put on a pink scarf once in a while."

Little B stops talking and looks at Rose as if to say, 'Did that answer your question?'

ROSE: What the fuck?

No response.

ROSE: Did you memorize that?

LITTLE B: "It's one of those things that maybe I'm too much in the middle of to describe."

ROSE: Okay, look, why don't you not talk for a minute? I have an idea.

LITTLE B: What kind of idea?

ROSE: Do you like Nine Inch Nails?

LITTLE B: I don't know.

ROSE: Have you ever heard it?

LITTLE B: I don't know what it is.

ROSE: You've never even heard of it?

LITTLE B: No.

ROSE: Okay. I'm gonna teach you something. Put your headphones on.

Little B puts her headphones on. Rose takes out her Walkman, opens it, and takes the CD out.

ROSE: This is Nine Inch Nails. Trent Reznor is God. You're gonna
　　　listen to this CD right now, okay?

> *Rose puts the Nine Inch Nails CD into*
> *Little B's Walkman.*

LITTLE B: Okay.
ROSE: I'll listen to your CD while you listen to mine. Then maybe
　　　we'll understand each other better. Okay?
LITTLE B: Okay.

> *Rose puts the Bjork CD into her*
> *Walkman. They both sit together,*
> *listening to each other's music.*
>
> *After about thirty seconds, BLACKOUT.*

SCENE THREE

LIGHTS UP on Rose, reading again.
("Go Ask Alice"? "The Bell Jar"?
"Please Kill Me: An Oral History of
Punk"? "The Lovely Bones"?)

KRISTEN (*from off*): Hello?

Kristen enters.

KRISTEN: Hi.

ROSE: Hi.

KRISTEN: The front door was open, so I...

ROSE: Okay.

Rose goes back to her journal.

KRISTEN: Where's your mom?

ROSE: Getting ready.

KRISTEN: Then I guess I'll wait here.

Beat.

I'm Kristen, by the way.

ROSE: I'm Rose.

KRISTEN: I know.

Beat.

ROSE: Why are you here?

KRISTEN: She didn't tell you I was coming?

ROSE: I don't know. Maybe.

KRISTEN: Your mom's dad is dying.

ROSE: I know.

KRISTEN: As soon as she's ready, we're going to pick her brother and sister up and then go to the hospital.

ROSE: You were giving her a lapdance, right?

KRISTEN: That was me.

ROSE: Are you a dyke?

KRISTEN: No.

ROSE: I'm pregnant.

KRISTEN: I heard.

ROSE: Do you think I'm too young?

KRISTEN: Yes. But I think *I'm* too young and I'm older than you, so don't think I'm judging you. I'm not.

ROSE: How old are you?

KRISTEN: None of your business.

ROSE: If you're a dyke, you don't have to worry about getting pregnant.

KRISTEN: Not true.

ROSE: Yes it is.

KRISTEN: If you're a dyke, you worry about not getting pregnant.

ROSE: Then you *are* a dyke?

KRISTEN: I let myself love who I love.

ROSE: What's that mean?

KRISTEN: No labels. If the person I love happens to be a woman...

ROSE: That makes you a dyke.

KRISTEN: You're not listening to me.

ROSE: Listen, what I saw that night—you and my mom—it freaked me out.

KRISTEN: I'm sorry.

ROSE: Let me finish. The last few days have been really weird.

KRISTEN: Because of what you saw?

ROSE: No. That's what's weird about it. Because seeing your mom receive a lapdance from some other woman should be a traumatic experience. But then I found out that I'm gonna have a baby. And that felt even weirder. And then I found out that I have this whole family that I never knew about. I mean, she never told me about any of them. So then I spent some time with my Uncle Elliot. And he's really weird. Then I had dinner with him and my Grandmother, who I never knew I had, and also my Aunt B, who thinks she's Bjork because she's, like, crazy. Like she's literally crazy. So that was weird. So, like, to find out that I come from this group of fucked up people when I used to think I hadn't come from anything, it makes some sort of sense. Now do you get what I'm trying to say about my mom?

KRISTEN: No.

ROSE: I think that if I found out my mom was a lesbian a week ago, I would have freaked out. But now it just seems, like, normal.

KRISTEN: You aren't how I expected you would be.

ROSE: No?

KRISTEN: Not from how your mom described you.

ROSE: How did she describe me?

KRISTEN: You're a lot more talkative than she makes you out to be, for one. And she thinks that you're depressed, or angry, or something that she can't really pinpoint even though she tries. She tries really hard...And she doesn't understand why you wear so much black. And she thinks that you're prettier than you let yourself be because you're always hiding behind so much make-up, and that...*I think*...is, you know, true. I'm sorry, I'll stop, I shouldn't be saying all of this. It's just that she talks about you a lot, and I had this picture of this, like, morose girl. Oh god that's not what I meant. That's me, not her. What I mean, here, this is...okay: When she talks about you, all of a sudden, it's like she becomes a different person...and she looks like a mother to me...and I guess it's kind of hard not to appreciate something so pure and instinctual. If I wasn't so sure of myself, I'd probably be jealous.

ROSE: Are you in love with her?

KRISTEN: I think I might be.

ROSE: You think?

KRISTEN: Well I haven't talked to her about it, but it's something that's crossed my mind.

ROSE: You should tell her.

KRISTEN: You think?

ROSE: Yeah.

Becky enters.

BECKY: Kristen, you're here.

KRISTEN: Hi.

BECKY: So you've met Rose, then?

KRISTEN: Officially.

ROSE: Do you two want me to leave or something?

BECKY: We should get to the hospital.

ROSE: But do you two, like, want a moment alone?

BECKY: We're fine.

ROSE: Kristen?

KRISTEN: Your mom's right. We should get to the hospital. Plenty of moments alone later.

BECKY: Rose, you're acting strange.

ROSE: I know, but I'm not. I mean, everything's actually cool.

BECKY: Then let's go.

ROSE: Wait. I have to get my journal.

She goes.

BECKY: Did she just say "everything's actually cool"?

KRISTEN: Yes.

BECKY: What did you do to her?

KRISTEN: We talked.

BECKY: You had a conversation?

KRISTEN: Yeah.

> *Becky goes to Kristen, kisses her.*

ROSE (*from off*): I'm coming back in!

> *Becky and Kristen break apart, like kids,*
> *almost caught.*

BECKY: Okay, let's go.

> *BLACKOUT.*

> *End of Act Four.*

ACT FIVE

SCENE ONE

Hospital Waiting Room: Mom, Elliot, Little B, Becky, Rose, and Kristen.

Waiting.

We finally see them all as a family—even Kristen, who though not blood, already feels an integral part of the whole— because, after all, they're all new to the idea of being a family again. And family is what we make it.

These are six people who feel damaged and—hope of all hopes—they're beginning to heal together.

The death of this man—this father—an almost ritualistic act.

These six people waiting like on New Years Eve for the ball to drop, for obligation to cease,

147

for hatred to melt away,
for wounds to heal,
for the future to bring something better,
for the moment when they look around
the room and it feels more like family
than regret.

Waiting.

To love. To remember that people are
beautiful. Can be. The joy of that.

All that said, this scene should be very
simple.

Six people waiting.

The whir of the air conditioner. Perhaps
we hear a hospital intercom request:
("Paging Dr. Glass. Paging Dr. Glass.")

Rose writes in her journal. Elliot shows
Rose that he's brought his as well, like
he had promised, so they can play the
game. Mom can't take her eyes off
Becky. Becky and Kristen share a candy

from the vending machine. Brooke and Elliot avoid each other (They first confronted the reality of their new situation together in the car on the way here. There's an unspoken understanding that right now *is not the right time, but Kristen will tell Becky about her past with Elliot later.) Little B has her Walkman, which she might or might not be listening to, and which might or might not still have NIN inside.*

This scene should be no longer than 60 seconds. Preferably shorter. A snapshot.

Dr. Stearn enters. The family turns to him, expectantly.

BLACKOUT.

SCENE TWO

Very late at night. Mom is in her nightgown. She picks up the phone and dials. In another part of the stage, a phone rings. Dr. Stearn, in his lab coat, answers the phone.

STEARN: This is Doctor Stearn.

MOM: Hi.

STEARN: Hello?

MOM: It's me.

STEARN: Who is this?

MOM: It's Rose.

STEARN: Rose?

MOM: Do you mind that I called this late?

STEARN: What time is it?

MOM: It's three in the morning.

STEARN: Well, it's a little—

MOM: It's late, isn't it?

STEARN: No, it's just that—

MOM: You're working, aren't you?

STEARN: Not really.

MOM: I only have this number.

STEARN: I'm off duty. I shouldn't be here.

MOM: You're not working?

STEARN: You're lucky you caught me.

MOM: You don't mind that I called?

STEARN: No, but could you please tell me who this is again?

MOM: Rose Silverstein.

STEARN: Oh, that's right.

MOM: You took care of my husband. He passed the other night.

STEARN: Yes.

MOM: I wanted to thank you.

STEARN: You're welcome.

MOM: For taking care of him. For letting him...

STEARN: It's all right.

MOM: For letting him...

STEARN: It's my job.

MOM: I know, but for helping him...

STEARN: It's what I do.

Beat.

STEARN: Are you still there?

MOM: I can't sleep ever since he went to the hospital. Have you
ever...Are you married, Dr. Stearn?

STEARN: No.

MOM: Have you ever been married?

STEARN: No.

MOM: Have you ever lost someone so close?

STEARN: Yes.

MOM: Who?

STEARN: My—.

He can't finish the thought.

MOM: Who?

STEARN: My...

*He doesn't say. He might be about to cry,
but he doesn't. He takes a breath and
pulls himself together.*

    Yes.

MOM: I see.

STEARN: Yeah.

MOM: You know, he raped all three of my kids?

STEARN: Who did?

MOM: My husband.

Beat. Silence.

MOM: Are you still there?

STEARN: I don't know what to—

MOM: Don't say anything. I just wanted to make sure you knew that.
    Because I—.

She stops. Beat.

STEARN: What?

MOM: I still loved him.

STEARN: Yeah?

MOM: There isn't another word to describe it.

Beat.

I'm a bad person.

Beat.

MOM: I should've left, but I couldn't because I didn't—

STEARN: Don't—

MOM: I didn't want to.

Beat.

STEARN: You're not a bad person.

MOM: No?

STEARN: No.

Beat.

MOM: I don't know who to believe anymore. But if my kids told me I was bad, I'd believe them. They're the only people who have absolute authority. If my oldest one—Becky—if she left again, it would kill me.

STEARN: How are they?

MOM: The kids...well, they're—.

Beat.

I think there's an overall sense of relief. Does that make sense?

STEARN: Yeah.

MOM: Little B doesn't seem much different, which is...upsetting. I was hoping she'd—.

Beat.

And, um, Becky is...happy. She was waiting for this. She's happy. And then Elliot. Elliot. You know, my house has been so empty lately—ever since Paul went to the hospital, it's...so quiet...Do you know what Elliot did last night? He came home. He hasn't been here since he took Little B away. That was three years ago. But last night...he was here. He didn't stay very long. He said it was something he needed to do, come inside again. I made cookies. We cried a little. And then he had to go pick up Little B from Becky's house.

Beat.

I think they'll be okay. I think they will...Are you still there?

STEARN: Yes.

MOM: Doctor, I am a fifty-five-year-old woman.

STEARN: Yes?

MOM: I don't know that I can get through the night.

STEARN: Is that why you're—

MOM: What?

STEARN: I could get you some Ambien. Or if you want something stronger...

MOM: No. I don't want sleeping pills.

STEARN: Oh, I'm sorry. Then, um—

MOM: Yes?

STEARN: Why did you call?

MOM: Do you mind if I cross the line, doctor?

STEARN: I guess not.

MOM: What are you wearing?

STEARN: White.

MOM: Your uniform?

STEARN: Yes.

MOM: Cotton?

STEARN: Yes.

MOM: I'm wearing a nightie.

STEARN: Oh.

MOM: Silk.

STEARN: Okay.

MOM: If I was with you right now, tell me what you'd—. What we would—. What would you want from me?

STEARN: I'm...

MOM: What?

STEARN: I'm afraid you'll think I'm weird.

MOM: You can say anything.

STEARN: Okay.

MOM: I won't judge you.

Beat.

STEARN: I'd want a sandwich.

MOM: What's that?

STEARN: I'm hungry.

MOM: With desire?

STEARN: When I'm up this late, I get hungry. If we were together right now, that's what I'd want.

MOM: You mean an actual "sandwich"?

STEARN: I'm sorry.

MOM: Fine.

STEARN: What?

MOM: Fine. I just need to see someone...You.

Mom and the doctor look at each other
for the first time.

STEARN: I don't know.

MOM: Tonight.

STEARN: It's late.

MOM: Come over.

STEARN: I shouldn't.

MOM: I'm the only one home. The emptiness is suffocating me.

STEARN: It's just—

MOM: Would you please just come over here? Now.

Lights shift. They cross to each other.
Mom holds a plate with a peanut butter
and jelly sandwich on it.

MOM: Hi.

STEARN: Hi.

MOM: Thank you for coming to see me. I know it's late.

STEARN: It's no problem.

MOM: Did you notice how summer came early this year?

STEARN: What do you mean?

MOM: It's just so hot.

STEARN: Is it?

MOM: It shouldn't be this hot this late at night this early in the year.

STEARN: I hadn't noticed.

Mom motions to her nightie.

MOM: Do you mind?

STEARN: I, um...

MOM: I didn't change out of my nightie.

STEARN: I see.

MOM: I hope you don't mind.

STEARN: I didn't think I should change because I'm a doctor.

Beat. Dr. Stearn eats the sandwich.

STEARN: It's a really good sandwich.

MOM: Thank you.

Beat.

MOM: Will you touch me?

STEARN: Where?

MOM: My husband never had to ask where.

STEARN: But what do you like?

MOM: Will you touch my breasts?

Dr. Stearn puts one hand on one breast.
After a moment, he takes it off.

MOM: We're not going to do anything, are we?

STEARN: No.

MOM: You don't like my body? Is it my—

STEARN: I'm gay.

MOM: How gay?

STEARN: Pretty gay.

MOM: Then why did you come to my house?

STEARN: You called so late. You sounded desperate. You sounded scared. You sounded like—

MOM: Stop, it's embarrassing.

STEARN: ...you needed someone.

MOM: I do.

Beat.

I don't know what to do now. I've wasted so much time. I don't want to feel this way. I don't know what to do with my life. What do I do? I know I need someone. I know that. I need someone so badly. Oh my God, dear God, I want someone to love me and fuck me and treat me right and love me and make love to me and love me. And I want it crude and real and messy and emotional, but good. I need someone and if you could be that person tonight—we don't even have to do things, you could just hold me—if you will let me pretend that this is something real—that this is *right*—if you will give me some hope—if you will just fucking touch me—just touch me—just love me—that's all I want. Just love me. I don't know what else to do, but maybe we can—can we start there?

STEARN: Are you done?

MOM: What do you mean?

STEARN: Making it about you.

MOM: I'm not—what? Why would you say that?

STEARN: Do you love your kids?

MOM: Of course I do.

STEARN: Then be there for them.

MOM: That's a given.

STEARN: Is it?

MOM: I'm their mom.

STEARN: That's all you have to do now. Be their fucking mom.

MOM: Why are you being hostile?

STEARN: What your husband did—

MOM: Don't talk about it.

STEARN: You didn't stop him.

MOM: What could I do?

STEARN: You could have left. You could have put the kids in the car
    and gotten out of there.

MOM: I couldn't.

STEARN: Keep telling yourself that.

MOM: I could give you a million excuses, but it won't change the fact
    that I didn't leave. There's nothing I can do to change that. I'll
    deal with it for the rest of my life. What I did...What I didn't
    do...all that's between me and my kids. You don't get to tell me
    how to feel. It's between me and them. This connection I have
    with my kids now, it's fragile. I know that. I'm afraid if I breathe
    too hard, I'll blow it all away. So I'm going to enjoy it while I

can. Now this thing between you and me, if you're not going to fuck me—

STEARN: I'm not gonna fuck you.

MOM: Then will you hold me?

STEARN: You want me to hold you?

MOM: Please.

STEARN: Okay.

MOM: Really?

STEARN: Yes.

MOM: Hold me like you love me.

BLACKOUT.

EPILOGUE.

Wake.

For the first time, the whole family is together in their old house. The father is in the ground and it's time to reclaim this space.

Becky and Kristen hold each other.

Little B throws car parts and cutlery off a precipice.

Elliot and Rose play the book game with their journals.

After a few moments, Mom enters with some sort of nourishment. (Maybe a jar of peanut butter and some spoons.)

No one speaks. It's enough just to be together.

After a few moments, Little B gets an idea. She puts "Post" into the stereo, and plays Track #4: "It's Oh So Quiet."

Little B may sing along. Sometimes to herself, sometimes to other members of her family. No one else should sing along (except maybe Elliot, if he feels like it, when Little B comes to him).

The family continues to comfort each other, appreciating the gift of the song.

At one point, Elliot might lay his head in Becky's lap.

Becky might comb her daughter's hair out of her eyes.

Rose and Kristen might have a giggle fit together.

Kristen might look through a family photo album with Mom.

Mom might sit, rapt, watching her youngest daughter sing.

Little B might make a peanut butter sandwich for her brother.

Etc.

The duration of this scene should be no more than five minutes. There should be no speaking and no pantomiming. It's simply a moment in which these people exist together without the necessity of words.

Finally, the lights dim to blackout, as the family continues on this new

beginning.

About the Playwright

ERIK PATTERSON is an award-winning playwright, screenwriter, and writing teacher.

His play, *One of the Nice Ones*, earned the Los Angeles Drama Critics Circle Award. His theater work has been produced or developed by Playwrights' Arena, the Los Angeles Theatre Centre, Theatre of NOTE, the Evidence Room, The Actors' Gang, the Echo Theater Company, the Lark Play Development Center, Moving Arts, Black Dahlia, Naked Angels, the Mark Taper Forum, and New Group. His plays have been nominated for the Ovation Award, the Stage Raw Award, the LA Weekly Award, and the GLAAD Media Award.

His writing for TV has been recognized with the Humanitas Prize and the Writer's Guild Award, as well as two Emmy nominations. Along with his writing partner, Jessica Scott, Erik has written films for Warner Bros., Universal, 20th Century Fox, Disney, Freeform, MTV, Paramount, Hallmark, and Syfy, among others. Film and TV credits include: *Abandoned* (starring Emma Roberts and Michael Shannon), *R.L. Stine's The Haunting Hour*, *Another Cinderella Story* (starring Selena Gomez and Jane Lynch), *Deep Blue Sea 2*, *Radio Rebel*, and many more.

Erik is a graduate of Occidental College and the British American Drama Academy. He hosts a gently-guided writing sprint online called "Sunday Sprints" that attracts writers seeking community and inspiration to do their best work.

www.erikpatterson.org

Plays by Erik Patterson

Tonseisha
drama / 1 female, 5 male / 45 minutes, no intermission
A young Japanese woman is haunted by the loss of two men: her father, whom she barely knew, and cult novelist Richard Brautigan, whom she never met. Akiko plays out her father/Richard Brautigan fantasies with a new man nearly every night. Each one of her relationships begins in a bar and ends in a bedroom, and she's never satisfied. She's so lost...can she ever be found?

Yellow Flesh / Alabaster Rose
dark comedy / 5 female, 4 male / full length, one intermission
Elliot is lost in a world of sex workers—late night house calls from hustlers and phone calls with call girls. Becky is torn between two worlds—her day job as a stripper and being a mom to fifteen-year-old Rose (a Goth girl who wants nothing to do with her). And then there's Little B, who has stripped away every piece of herself until all she has left is her obsession with Icelandic pop singer Bjork. This troubled family's shared past holds unspeakable horrors and they must join forces if they ever want to heal. *Winner of the Backstage West Garland Award for Best Playwriting.*

Red Light, Green Light
drama / 6 female, 7 male / full length, one intermission
A gay clown. Two lesbian strippers. A pregnant Goth teen. A deadbeat dad. A horny mother. And a girl who thinks she's Bjork. In this stand-alone sequel to *Yellow Flesh / Alabaster Rose*, the Silverstein family journey towards healing is abruptly halted when Elliot becomes the victim of a brutal gay bashing.

He Asked For It
drama / 1 female, 6 male / full length, one intermission
It's the early 2000s, before PrEP. Ted is new to Los Angeles, and newly out of the closet. He goes on a journey through Hollywood back rooms, nightclub bathrooms, and Internet chat rooms—where he meets and falls in love with Henry. But Henry doesn't yet know how to navigate the dating landscape with his new HIV diagnosis, so he breaks things off with Ted...who then makes a desperate decision to win Henry back. *He Asked For It* asks how far are you willing to go for love? And how much will you forgive? *GLAAD Media Award nominee for Outstanding Los Angeles Theater.*

Sick

dramedy / 3 female, 3 male, 1 child / full length, no intermission
David needs to get laid, Gary could use a drink, and Tim would like you to take your top off. Carla craves cocaine, Jeannie's got God, and Pamela keeps digging herself deeper into the funny and frightening world of hypochondria. But when one of their own gets sick for real, they're all going to have to face their greatest fears and grow up.

I Wanna Hold Your Hand

dramedy / 3 female, 3 male / full length, no intermission
Our lives can change in an instant. One moment you're getting engaged, and a few surreal moments later you're sitting with strangers in an ICU waiting room, praying your fiancé will survive a brain aneurysm. While waiting for Frank to wake from a coma, Ada meets Julia, Paul, and Josh, who are waiting for their mom to wake up. A tenuous friendship is born. *I Wanna Hold Your Hand* looks at life, death, and recovery, and what it means to try your hand at living again...

One of the Nice Ones

dark comedy / 2 female, 2 male / 90 minutes, no intermission
A paraplegic woman plays outrageous power games to get something she desperately wants in this dark, twisty, sexy play that takes office politics to new extremes. *Winner of the Los Angeles Drama Critics Circle Award for Best Playwriting.*

Handjob

dark comedy / 2 female, 4 male / 90 minutes, no intermission
An encounter between a white, gay playwright and his black, straight "shirtless maid" goes disastrously wrong when signals are misinterpreted, lines crossed. *Handjob* explores the aftermath of their meeting, as it reveals deep layers of discrimination, discord, and discontent among people who should be allies. How do you know when you've gone too far if you completely ignore other people's boundaries?

167

Books by Erik Patterson

Pop Prompts: 200 Writing Prompts Inspired by Popular Music
Available in paperback and e-book

Pop Prompts is a collection of writing prompts that will help you dig deeper and break through creative blocks. Each prompt is paired with a pop song. Let the music be your muse as you work on your memoir, novel, script, poem—or even your own songs. This book can also be a daily jumpstart for therapeutic journaling. Use it however you want, whenever you want. As long as you're writing you're doing it right.

Pop Prompts For Swifties: 99 Writing Prompts
Available in paperback and e-book

Every writing prompt in this book is paired with one of Taylor's songs from the first "era" of her storytelling journey, from her debut album *Taylor Swift* (2006), to *Fearless* (2008), to *Speak Now* (2010), to *Red* (2012), and all the way through *1989* (2014). You don't even have to be a Swiftie—anyone can use these prompts for self-expression and reflection. As a bonus, each prompt includes blank journal pages. Inspiration is only a song away. Put on your favorite Taylor Swift album, pick a prompt, and start writing! Taylor Swift has no involvement in this book. The use of her name is merely descriptive and should not be interpreted as a sign of endorsement.

SUNDAY SPRINTS

Need some motivation?

Do you work better when someone is holding you accountable?

Come to SUNDAY SPRINTS.

Erik Patterson hosts gently-guided writing sprints on Zoom every Wednesday from 6 to 8 p.m. PST and every Sunday from noon to 2 p.m. PST. (Yes, it's called Sunday Sprints on Wednesdays because... why not?)

Here's how it works: I give a new writing prompt every fifteen minutes. You write. That's it.

All sprinters stay on mute. Alone but not alone, you can draw creative energy from the community of writers on your screen. This is a fun, low-pressure environment—a safe space for you to experiment with your writing. No worries: I will never ask you to share your work.

You decide how to use this distraction-free writing time. Work on that screenplay, novel, short story, play, poem, song. Do some therapeutic journaling. Write letters to loved ones. Do some technical writing. Create a D&D campaign. Finish your homework. Seriously, whatever you need to work on.

Let's get that writing done. Together.

Join the Sunday Sprints Patreon at:
www.patreon.com/erikpatterson

Subscribe to the Sunday Sprints mailing list at:
www.erikpatterson.org/sundaysprints

www.ingramcontent.com/pod-product-compliance
Lightning Source LLC
Chambersburg PA
CBHW070707130626
46553CB00005B/1880